Viv Lambert and
Cheryl

Preparation for the A2 Flyers
Cambridge English Qualifications

Student's Book

with Digital Graded Reader

The pleasure of learning

Contents

Welcome!

1 🔊1 Look and listen. Then complete.

fourteen • April • nineteenth • ~~ten~~ • twenty-first

Sarah Hi! My name's Sarah. I'm __ten__.
George I'm ten, too! When's your birthday?
Sarah It's in (**1**) ____________. It's on the (**2**) ____________.
George Mine is on the (**3**) ____________ of April. I'm older than you!
Max is two. That's (**4**) ____________ in dog years.
Sarah He's older than both of us!

2 🔊2 Listen and write the number. Say the months.

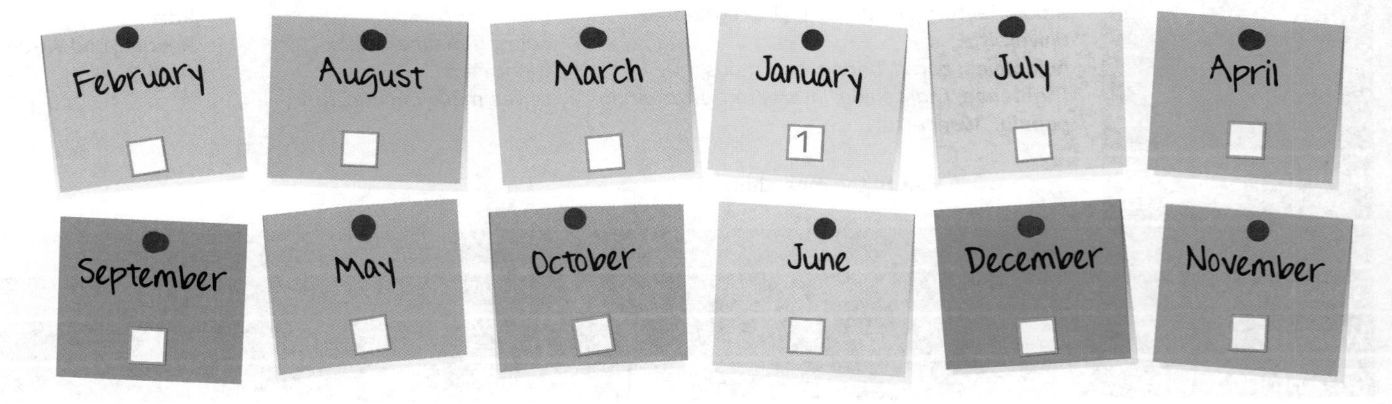

Look & Learn

When's your birthday?
It's **in** April.
It's **on** the first of April.

3 Write the ordinal numbers. Then listen and check.

4 Say the Sounds Listen and say this three times.

Sally's birthday is on the thirtieth of September.

5 Listen and write. When are their birthdays?

6 Say & Play Find somebody whose birthday is

	Name
in the same month as yours.	
in a month beginning with 'J'.	
this month.	

When's your birthday?

It's on the 12th of March.

1 It isn't in my room!

1 🔊 6 **Look, listen and point. What's for dinner?**

2 🔊 7 **Write the numbers. Listen, check and say.**

shelf	7	oven	☐
shampoo	☐	fridge	☐
soap	☐	diary	☐
cushion	☐	brush	☐
cooker	☐	comb	☐

3 🔊 8 **Write the words from exercise 2. Listen, check and say.**

1 It's in the bathroom.

shelf ______ ______ ______

2 It's in the bedroom.

______ ______ ______ ______

3 It's in the kitchen.

______ ______ ______

4 9 **Find these things in the picture on page 6. Then write the words. Listen, check and say.**

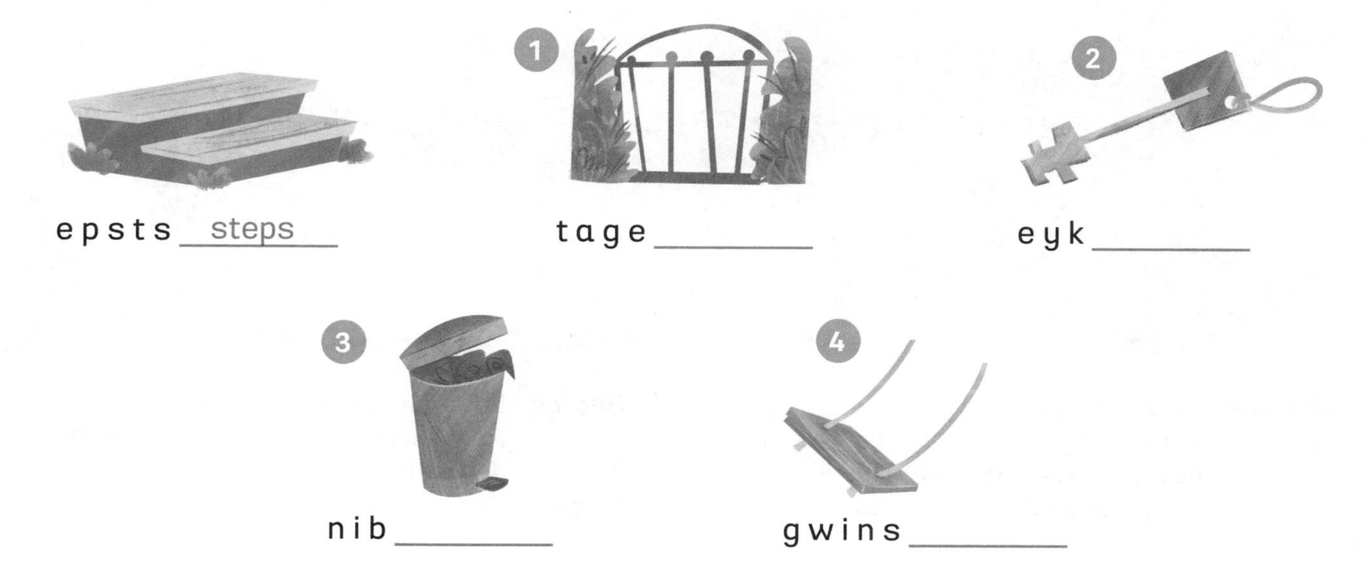

epsts steps

1 tage ________

2 eyk ________

3 nib ________

4 gwins ________

5 **Student A, look at this picture. Student B, look at the picture on page 125. Find six differences.**

In picture A, there are three steps.

In Picture B, there are five steps.

6 Say & Play **Cut out and play. Guess the word.**

You're washing your hands. It's soap!

Yes! You're right.

It isn't in my room!

7 **Listen and read. What two things does George make?**

George What are you doing?
Sarah I'm making some dolls. And this is the house where they live! This is the living room where they watch TV.

George Let's cut this into two squares. Look. Now these are cushions where the dolls sit!
Sarah Great idea!

Sarah What are you making?
George A cooker. Look. When you open the door, there's an oven!
Sarah That's fantastic!

George This is the house where I'd like to live! But how do the people get inside?
Sarah Oh no! I forgot to make a door!

8 Look and rewrite.

My friend lives in this house.
This is the house where my friend lives.

1 I live in this street.
This is the street ________________.

2 I sit here and write my diary.
This is the place ________________.

3 We always go on holiday here.
This is the place ________________.

4 My dog sleeps here.
This is ________________.

Look & Learn

This is the house **where** they live.
This is the living room **where** they watch TV.
These are the cushions **where** the dolls sit.

where clause p. 137

9 Choose and write.

Where • When • Who • How • Why • ~~What~~ • Which

Helen Hello! Are you the new people in flat 9?
Oliver Yes, we are! My name's Oliver. What 's your name?
Helen I'm Helen. I live at number 6. (**1**) ________ did you move to your new flat?
Oliver Yesterday. (**2**) ________ do you go to school?
Helen Woodpark School.
Oliver Oh, that's my new school. Do you like it there?
Helen Yes, it's a great school. (**3**) ________ class are you in?
Oliver I'm in Class 4.
Helen Me too! That's the best class!
Oliver (**4**) ________?
Helen Because we've got a really nice teacher.
Oliver (**5**) ________ is the teacher?
Helen Her name's Miss Green.
Oliver (**6**) ________ do you get to school?
Helen I walk. It's just a few streets from here. We can walk together on Monday.
Oliver Yes, thanks. I'd like that.

10 11 Write the questions. Then match. Listen and check.

Who is your best friend? c
1 ________ do you like your best friend? ☐
2 ________ is your birthday? ☐
3 ________ do you do in your free time? ☐
4 ________ do you get to school? ☐
5 ________ subject do you like best? ☐
6 ________ do you want to travel to one day? ☐

a Maths.
b It's on 31st May.
~~c~~ His name's David.
d Because he's funny!
e I read.
f I go by bike.
g I'd like to visit London!

11 Say & Play Talk with a friend. Ask and answer the questions in exercise 10.

FLYERS PRACTICE

Reading and Writing Part 1

There are some words you don't need to use.

1 Look and read. Choose the correct words and write them on the lines. There is one example.

an oven **a fridge** **a diary** **shampoo** **a desk** **a brush** **cushions** **soap** **a shelf** **a comb** **a key** **steps** **a swing** **a gate** **a cooker**

It's the place where you put a cake or a chicken to cook. oven

1 You find it in the bathroom. You wash your hands with it. ________

2 You use it to wash your hair. ________

3 You can open a door or a gate with this. ________

4 It's usually on a wall. You can put books or CDs on it. ________

5 You find this in the kitchen. You cook pasta or soup on it. ________

6 You can find it in a playground. Children play on it. ________

7 They are usually outside a building. You walk up or down them. ________

8 You keep butter and milk here. It keeps food cold. ________

9 It's got a page for every day. You write the homework you have to do. ________

10 It's usually in a wall around a building or garden. You open it when you want to go into a place. ________

Listening Part 3

2 12 **What did each person buy on holiday? Listen and write a letter in each box. There is one example.**

Listen to the whole dialogue before you choose the correct picture.

Michael [E]

his mum [ ]

his dad [ ]

Betty [ ]

his grandpa [ ]

his grandma [ ]

Hide the biscuits!

1 🔊13 **Look, listen and point. What do they take to the tree house?**

2 🔊14 **Write the numbers. Listen, check and say.**

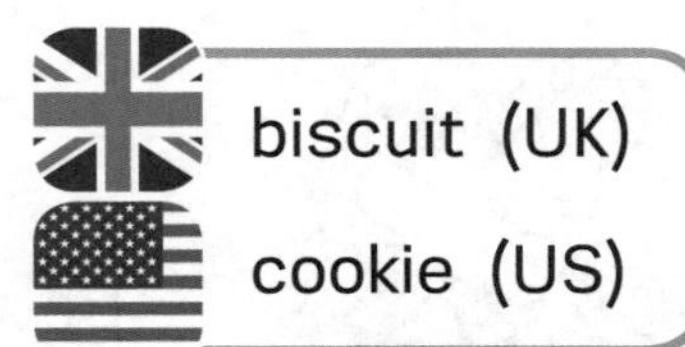

biscuits	1	flour	
sugar		olives	
cereal		pizza	
jam		strawberries	
butter		honey	
yoghurt			

3 🔊15 **Write the words. Listen and check.**

You can put it in your tea or coffee. sugar

1 They are small and black or green. They grow on trees. ________

2 They are red. They are a kind of fruit. ________

3 It's yellow. You can put it on bread, with honey. ________

4 It's made with fruit. You can put it on your bread. ________

5 You can make them with chocolate. Mmmm! ________

4 🔊16 Find and write. Then listen and check. Say the words.

~~glass~~ • salt • pepper • plate • knife • spoon • chopsticks • fork

Look & Learn

a glass	three glasses
a chopstick	two chopsticks
a knife	two knives

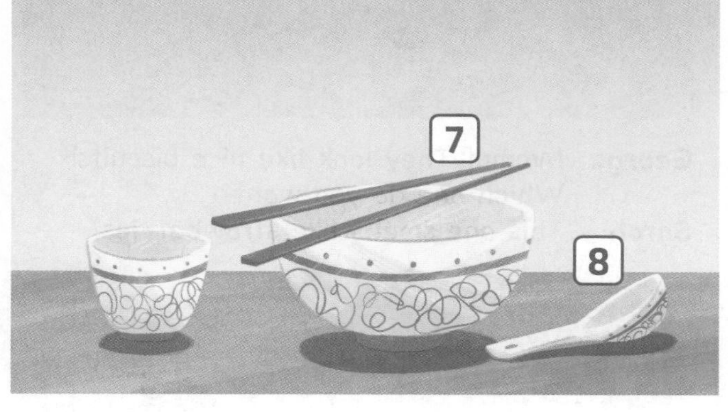

1 glass
2 ______
3 ______
4 ______
5 ______
6 ______
7 ______
8 ______

5 🔊17 Listen and tick (✔).

1 What do they have on their sandwiches?

A 
B 
C 

2 What's on the pizzas?

A 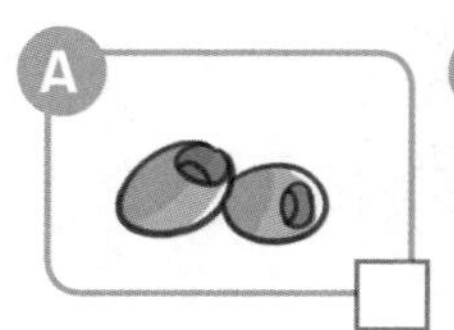
B 
C 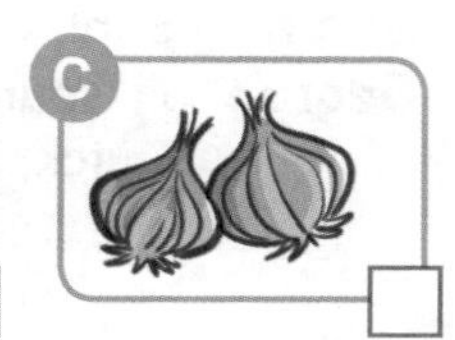

3 What else do they take to the picnic?

A 

B 
C 

4 What does Katy forget?

A 
B 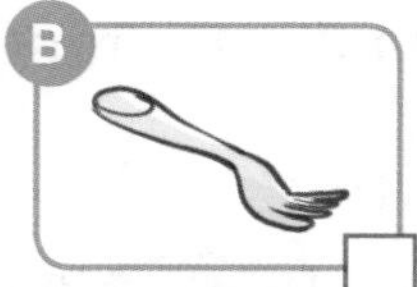
C 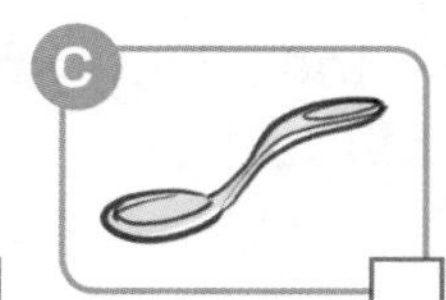

6 Say & Play Make a sentence and add a new word.

Look & Learn

a cake, some strawberries, some jam

I went to the market and I bought some jam.

I went to the market and I bought some jam and some strawberries.

I went to the market and I bought some jam, some strawberries and a cake.

Hide the biscuits!

7 18 Listen and read. Who has got the biscuits?

George Mmmm. They look like nice biscuits! Which one do you want?
Sarah This one smells like strawberries.

Sarah What's that one like? Is it nice?
George Yes, it tastes like chocolate. Shh! Max. They aren't dog biscuits.

Ben George! Where are you?
Sarah Shh! I can hear someone.
George It sounds like my brother. Quick, hide the biscuits.

Ben Oh, here you are! Mum can't find the biscuits. It's very strange ...
George We haven't got them.
Sarah Max! Get down!
George Oh, sorry! Max has got the biscuits!

8 Choose and write.

look like • ~~smell like~~ • taste like • sound like

Look & Learn

What's it like? It **tastes like** chocolate.
It **sounds like** my brother.
They **look like** nice biscuits.

p. 137

Mmm. It smells like flowers.

1 This ice cream __________ strawberries.

2 Ha ha! This phone __________ a bird!

3 That cloud __________ a dolphin.

9 19 Choose and write. Listen and check.

Shall we • See you later • Good idea
What's it like • ~~Shall I~~

Holly I'm hungry.
Robert Shall I find a snack for us?
Holly Yes, please. What's in the fridge?
Robert There's a cheese pie. Would you like that?
Holly I don't know. (1) ____________?
Robert It's delicious!
Holly (2) ____________ take it on a picnic?
Robert (3) ____________! Let's ride our bikes to the park.
Holly OK. I'll go and get my bike. Bye!
Robert (4) ____________!

Look & Learn

Shall I buy some snacks?
Yes, please!
Shall we make a cake?
Good idea!

▶ *shall* p. 137

10 Put the words in order. Then match and say.

1 snacks? / some / we / Shall / buy
____

2 a picnic / park? / Shall / in / we / the / have
____

3 film? / Shall / watch / we / a
____

4 sandwich? / on / put / Shall / jam / I / your
____

5 Shall / cake? / we / a / make
____

6 carry / Shall / I / bag? / your
____

a Not today. It's raining.
b No, we can't. We haven't got any flour.
c Oh, thank you! It's really heavy.
d Yes, please. I'm hungry.
e Good idea! Let's go to the cinema.
f Yes, please. Here's a knife.

11 Say & Play Student A, look at the card below. Student B, look at the card on page 125. Talk with a friend.

Student A

Say hello	Hello / Hi (*name*)
Suggest an activity	Shall we ... have a picnic / go to the park / go to the cinema?
Offer to bring something	Shall I bring ... a cake / some biscuits / some water?
Suggest a time	Let's meet ... today / tomorrow / Friday.
Say goodbye	OK. See you later / tomorrow / on Friday.

2 FLYERS PRACTICE

Listening Part 2

1 20 **Listen and write. There is one example.**

Look carefully at the gaps before you listen. What kind of information do you think you need to find?

COOKING CLUB

	Meet at:	4 o'clock on Wednesdays
1	The cook's name is:	Mrs ______________
2	Learn how to cook:	______________ and cakes
3	Children can bring:	tomatoes and ______________
4	Number of children:	______________
5	Finishes at:	______________ o'clock

Speaking Part 3

2 21 **Look at the pictures.**
Listen and continue to tell the story.

A HOT DAY

3 **Now watch the video and talk about your answers.**

3 This is your invitation!

1 22 **Look, listen and point. When is the street party?**

2 23 **Write the numbers. Listen, check and say.**

husband	1	stamp	
envelope		post	
wife		invitation	
post office		Dear	

3 24 **Find the words. Then read and complete. Listen and check.**

invitationstamppostofficedearenvelope

You write an invitation when you want to invite someone to a party.

1 Start like this: __________ Sam, ...

2 Put the invitation in an __________.

3 Now put a __________ on it.

4 Take it to the __________ __________.

4 Read and complete. Then listen and check. Say the words.

25

address • middle • members • telephone • surname • ~~letter~~

28 Park Road
Newington
01934 792501

Dear Smith family,
Richard and I got married in April! We had a very small party with only a few members of our families. But now we want to have a big party at our new home. Please come! It's in July and it starts at 3 o'clock. I hope you can come.
Best wishes
Grace Mary Roberts and Richard Jones

This is a letter from Grace.

1 She is writing to ________ of the Smith family.
2 Her ________ name is Mary.
3 Her husband's first name is Richard, and his ________ is Jones.
4 Their ________ is 28 Park Road, Newington.
5 Their ________ number is 01934 792501.

5 Circle the correct words.

A (letter) / envelope arrived yesterday. It was in a beautiful white (1) stamp / envelope with balloons on it. It had our family's (2) surname / first name – Smith – on it. My dad opened it and read it to us. "Your Aunt Grace got (3) invited / married!" he said. "She and her (4) wife / husband, Richard, are inviting all the (5) members / children of our family to a party at their new home." My dad pointed to the (6) invitation / address in Newington. "When is the party?" I asked. "Hmm. Aunt Grace forgot to tell us that! But she gave us her (7) post office / telephone number. Let's phone and ask her."
I'm so excited. I love parties!

6 Say & Play Play with a friend. Student B, turn to page 125. Find five differences.

3 This is your invitation!

7 Listen and read. Where is the party?

Sarah What shall I do with the balloons?
George You could put them on the tree, or you could give one to everyone at the party!

George We've only got ten glasses.
Sarah We could use some glasses from our houses.
George Good idea. Let's run home and get them.

Sarah Now we've got lots of glasses. And sausages!
George Yum! The food looks delicious.

George Oh no, Max!
Sarah He thinks the food's delicious, too!

Look & Learn

You **could put** them on the tree.
We **could use** some glasses from our houses.

▶ *could* p. 137

8 Choose and write.

go • make • fly • have • carry • ~~write~~

I want to tell my friends about my party.
You could write invitations.

1 I'm hungry.
You ________________ a snack.

2 What can I give my mum for Mother's Day?
You ________________ a card.

3 It's a sunny day. What shall we do?
We ________________ a kite.

4 I'm tired.
You ________________ to bed early.

5 How can I be kind to Grandma?
We ________________ the shopping.

9 27 Choose. Listen and check.

Katy It's my birthday soon! Mum says I can have a party.
I could / **What about** ask everyone in our class to come.

Ben Oh, what a great idea!

Katy Let's make some invitations. (1) **We could** / **How about** invite our teacher, too. Can you help me finish the invitations tomorrow after school?

Ben (2) **Yes, of course.** / **Sorry, I can't.**
I have to go shopping with my mum after school tomorrow.

Katy (3) **What about** / **You could** on Saturday?

Ben Yes, Saturday is fine.

Katy (4) **How about** / **Let's** do that then!

10 Match 1-4 with the answers A-D.

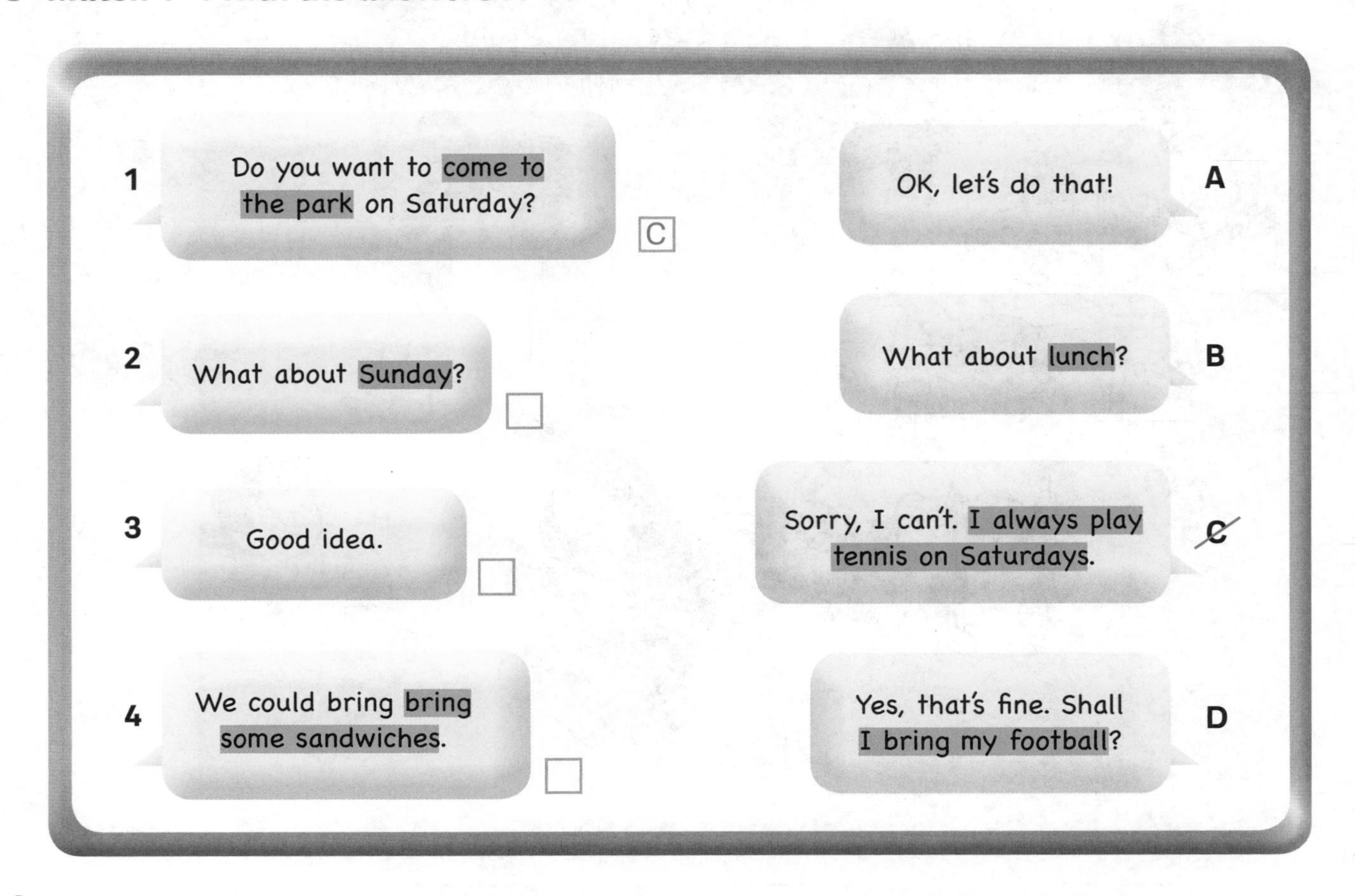

11 Say & Play Change the words in purple in exercise 10 and talk with a friend.

FLYERS PRACTICE

Listening Part 1

1 28 **Listen and draw lines. There is one example.**

Look carefully at the names before you listen. Which are boys' names? Which are girls' names?

Reading and Writing Part 2

Read all the sentences in the box before you choose your answer.

2 It's Katy's birthday party next weekend. She and her friend, Emma, are talking about the party. What does Katy say?
Read the conversation and choose the best answer. Write a letter (A-H) for each answer. You do not need to use all the letters. There is one example.

Example

Emma: How many people did you invite?

Katy: G

Questions

1 **Emma:** Did you phone them all?
Katy: ______

2 **Emma:** How did you send them?
Katy: ______

3 **Emma:** Now we need to think about the food!
Katy: ______

4 **Emma:** I could help you with that.
Katy: ______

5 **Emma:** Yes. Mine, too.
Katy: ______

A No, I sent them all invitations.
B OK, let's do that!
C I wrote their names and surnames.
D Thanks! What about a banana cake? That's my favourite.
E Sorry, I can't.
F Yes. We could make a cake!
G 20! I sent invitations to everyone in our class. **(example)**
H I posted them at the post office.

Let's dress up!

1 🔊29 **Look, listen and point. What does Sarah look like?**

2 🔊30 **Write the numbers. Listen, check and say.**

uniform	4	trainers	☐
sunglasses	☐	crown	☐
spotted pyjamas	☐	striped T-shirt	☐
umbrella	☐	belt	☐
necklace	☐	gloves	☐

3 🔊31 **Look and write. Then listen and check.**

1 George is wearing a gold crown and a big __________.
2 Sammy is wearing __________ __________, __________ and __________.
3 Sarah is wearing her school __________.
4 Her mum's wearing __________ and a __________.
5 Tom is wearing a __________ T-shirt.
6 Jill is carrying a huge __________.

4 32 Read and choose. Then listen and say.

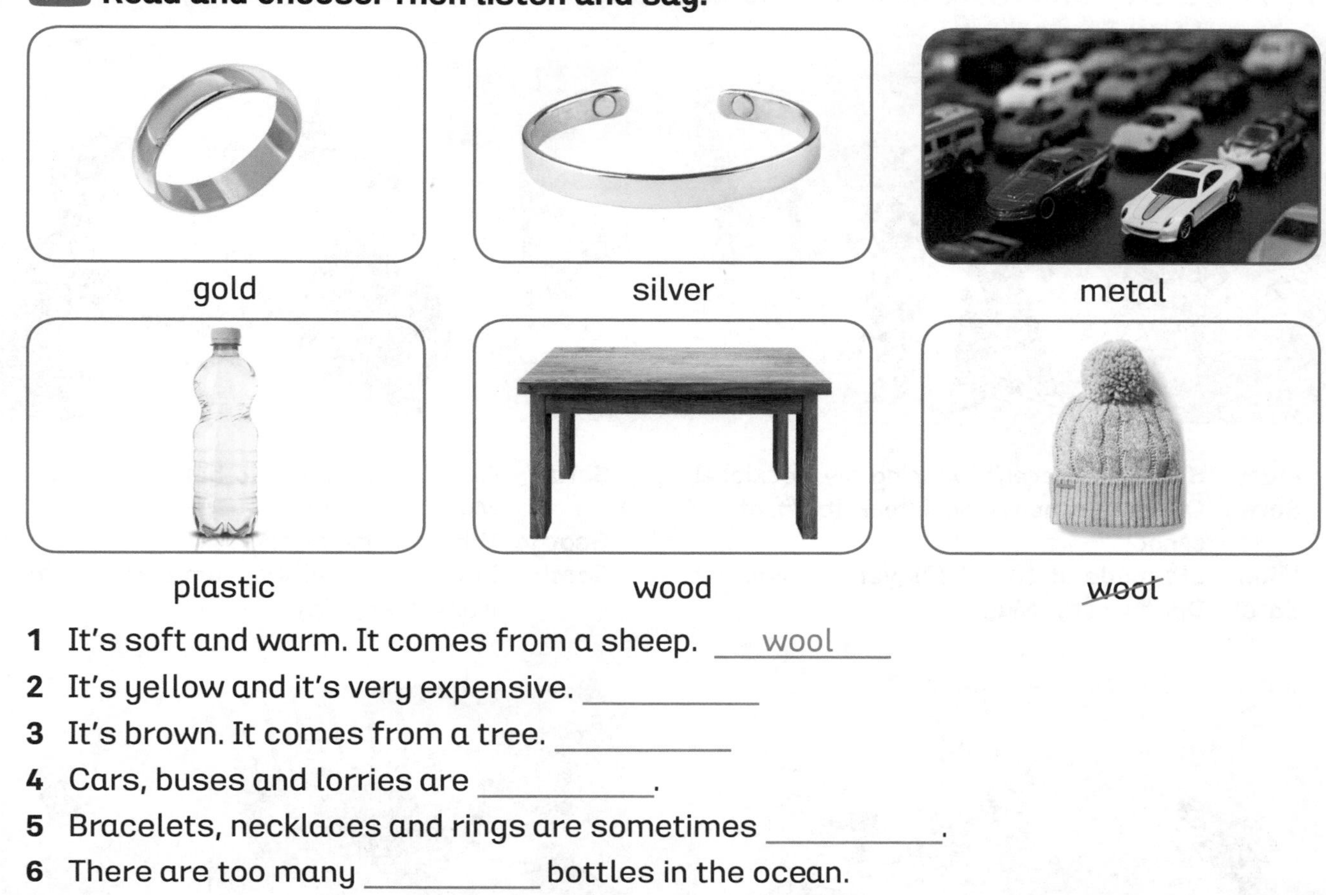

1 It's soft and warm. It comes from a sheep. wool
2 It's yellow and it's very expensive. ___________
3 It's brown. It comes from a tree. ___________
4 Cars, buses and lorries are ___________.
5 Bracelets, necklaces and rings are sometimes ___________.
6 There are too many ___________ bottles in the ocean.

5 33 Listen and write the names. There are two pictures you do not need.

Betty | Katy | ~~Frank~~ | Helen | Harry

6 Say & Play Play *Who am I?* Use the pictures in exercise 5.

Are you wearing sunglasses?

No, I'm not.

Let's dress up!

7 34 Listen and read. Who has the necklace?

Mum Sarah, you aren't wearing my necklace!
Sarah Oh, it was heavy so I took it off at school.
Mum It's made of silver! It's very expensive!
Sarah Don't worry, Mum.

Sarah George, you have to help me find Mum's necklace.
George What's it made of?
Sarah It's made of silver. Mum wears it to work every day.

Sarah Look, George! There's Max!
George Oh no! He's wearing your mum's necklace. Quick!

Sarah Max, stop! That necklace isn't made of plastic!
Mum Here's my necklace! Good boy, Max.

8 35 Look. Ask and answer. Then listen and check.

Look & Learn

What's it **made of**?
It's **made of** silver. It **isn't made of** plastic.

▶ *made of* p. 137

1 

2 

3 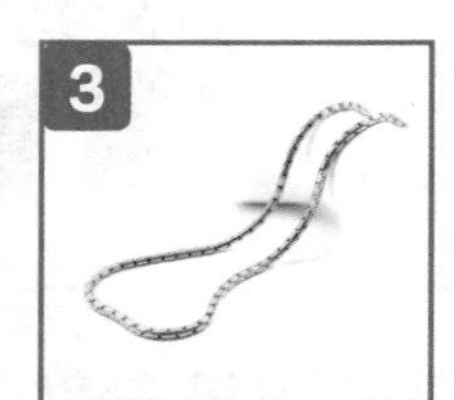

4 

5 

6 

It's made of gold. What is it?

It's a ring.

9 Listen. Then write *Yes* or *No*.

Look & Learn

I'm **wearing** a necklace today.
I **don't usually wear** a necklace.

Sally is wearing a dress. Yes
1 She usually wears dresses. ______
2 She usually wears necklaces. ______
3 The necklace is made of gold. ______
4 Robert is wearing a bracelet. ______
5 It's made of plastic. ______
6 He wears it every day. ______

Look & Learn

Use the **Present simple** with:
every day / **every night** / **usually** / **always** / **sometimes** / **never**

Use the **Present continuous** with:
now / **today**

Present simple v Present continuous p. 138

10 Circle the correct words.

Sarah's mum **goes** / **is going** to work every day.
1 Sarah **doesn't usually wear** / **isn't wearing** her mum's necklace now.
2 George **doesn't wear** / **isn't wearing** a crown every day.
3 Max **wears** / **is wearing** the necklace now.
4 Sophie **wears** / **is wearing** her pyjamas every night.
5 Jill is **carrying** / **carries** an umbrella today.

11 Now write four sentences about you.

Today I'm wearing ______
I usually wear ______
I don't usually wear ______
My favourite clothes are ______

FLYERS PRACTICE

Speaking Part 1

1 37 **Find the differences.**

Look carefully at the clothes, colours and numbers of things in the picture.

2 **Now watch the video and talk about your answers.**

Listening Part 5

3 38 **Listen and colour and write. There is one example.**

Listen carefully and only colour the things you are told to colour.

REVISION 0-4

1 **What's wrong? Find six more mistakes.**

There are brushes and combs on the tree.

2 **Circle the odd word.**

1	honey	butter	jam	plate
2	belt	envelope	necklace	glove
3	umbrella	cooker	fridge	oven
4	silver	metal	knife	wool
5	knife	fork	flour	spoon
6	chopsticks	pizza	yoghurt	biscuits

3 **Watch the video. Then circle the words.**

1 There is something in the tree and it **smells** / **looks** like a house.
2 Sarah has a tree house **that** / **where** they play.
3 The tree house is **made** / **make** of wood.
4 George **is wearing** / **wears** a crown today.
5 George's birthday is **in** / **on** 19th April.
6 They **could** / **can** have a party in the tree house.
7 George says '**Do** / **Shall** we ask Sarah?'

4 Say & Play **Ask and answer questions about the story.**

THE WRONG ADDRESS

My favourite subject!

1 🔊39 Look, listen and point. What's Sarah's favourite subject?

2 🔊40 Write the numbers. Listen, check and say.

gym	7		
rucksack	☐	history	☐
maths	☐	science	☐
geography	☐	timetable	☐
art	☐	dictionary	☐

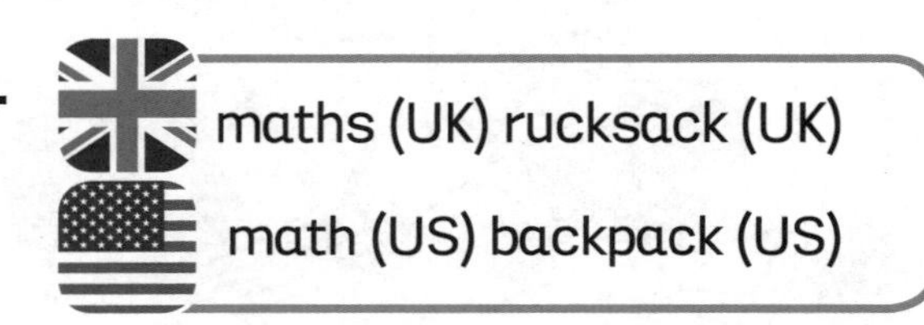

3 🔊41 Write the words. Listen and check.

You learn to use numbers in this subject. maths

1 You draw and paint in this class. ____________
2 It's a book that helps you understand words. ____________
3 You learn about the past in this class. ____________
4 It's a big room where you do sport. ____________
5 You can carry your books in this. ____________

4 🔊42 Say the Sounds Listen and say.

George has got geography but not in the gym.

5 43 **Look and write the same time. Then listen and check. Say the times.**

three thirty • ~~eight forty-five~~
midday • midnight • one fifteen p.m.

Look & Learn

a.m.	in the morning
p.m.	in the afternoon, evening or night
midday	12 o'clock in the day
midnight	12 o'clock at night

1 

2 

3 

4 

quarter to nine ___eight forty-five___
1 quarter past one ______________
2 half past three ______________
3 twelve a.m. ______________
4 twelve p.m. ______________

6 44 **Listen and complete the timetable.**

Monday	
9:00	science
10:30	break
1 ______________	history
11:30	art
2 ______________	lunch
3 ______________	English
4 ______________	geography
5 ______________	after-school club

7  Say & Play **Play the game.**

It's quarter to seven.

8 45 **Listen and read. What does Sarah want to do at 9 a.m.?**

George Hey, Sarah. Don't forget it's the art club trip to the museum tomorrow.
Sarah Oh yes. I love art! What time does the bus usually leave?
George It always leaves at half past eight. We mustn't be late.
Sarah OK, I must get up early! See you tomorrow.

The next morning...
Sarah Hey, George! Do we have to wear our uniform today?
George No, we don't have to wear our uniform, but don't forget, we have to bring something to eat for lunch.
Sarah OK! I must go and make my lunch.

Sarah Oh no! We're early! The museum is closed!
Teacher Good morning. What time does the museum open?

Teacher OK, children. The museum opens at half past nine.
Sarah We've got 30 minutes. Let's have lunch!
Teacher Sarah! It's nine o'clock in the morning!
Sarah I know, but I didn't have time for breakfast.

9 **Look at the sign. Write the questions. Then ask and answer.**

OPENING HOURS

MUSEUM	CAFÉ
Monday – Saturday:	Monday – Saturday:
9:30 am – 6:30 pm	10:15 am – 4:30 pm
Sunday: 12:30 pm – 5:00 pm	Sunday: 12:45 pm – 4:15 pm

Look & Learn

What time does the bus leave?
It leaves at half past eight.

museum / open / Tuesdays? What time does the museum open on Tuesdays?
1 café / close / Thursdays? ____
2 museum / close / Fridays? ____
3 café / open / Sundays? ____
4 museum / open / Sundays? ____

10 46 Choose and write. Then listen and check.

subjects • finishes
have to • does • mustn't
~~morning~~ • start • have to

Look & Learn

We **have to** clean the tables.
We **don't have to** go to school on Saturdays.
I **must get** up early.
We **mustn't be** late.

Dear Grace,
I want to tell you about my school. School starts at 8.30 in the morning. We **(1)** __________ be late. We **(2)** __________ wear our uniform to school every day. My favourite **(3)** __________ are maths and music. Lunch is at half past twelve. We eat our lunch in the classroom. We usually have rice, fish and soup. After lunch we **(4)** __________ clean the tables. Lessons **(5)** __________ again at half past one. School **(6)** __________ at quarter past three. After school we stay for clubs where we can play games or do music, art or sport. We go to school from Monday to Friday. We don't have to go to school on Saturdays! 🙂 Write to me and tell me about your school. What time **(7)** __________ it start? What do you eat for lunch and what do you have to wear?

From Yoko

11 Read Yoko's email again and write T (true) or F (false).

School starts at half past eight. T
1 They don't have to wear a uniform. ____
2 Yoko likes music. ____
3 Lunch is at one thirty. ____
4 After lunch they have to clean the tables. ____
5 They go home at three fifteen. ____
6 They have to go to school at the weekend. ____

12 Now answer these questions about you.

1 What time does school start?
2 Do you have to wear a uniform?
3 What do you eat for lunch?
4 What's your favourite subject?
5 What mustn't you do at school?
6 What time does school finish?
7 Do you have to go to school on Saturdays?

Listening Part 2

1 47 Listen and write. There is one example.

SPECIAL DAY AT SCHOOL

	Subject:	art
1	Art teacher:	Mr ______________
2	Wear:	______________ clothes
3	Bring:	plastic bottles, paper cups and ______________
4	Lunch:	12:30 to ______________
5	Art show	in the ______________

Speaking Part 2

2 48 **Ask questions to find the missing information. Student A look at this page, Student B look at page 126.**

Think about the questions you need to ask before you start.

Student A

Robert's favourite place

Favourite place	?
Where	?
Time open	?
Like doing	?
When	?

Holly's favourite place

Favourite place	sports centre
Where	opposite school
Time open	7:30 a.m.
Like doing	swimming
When	after school

Speaking Part 4

3 Ask and answer the questions with your partner.

1. Which subjects are the easiest?
2. Which subjects are difficult?
3. What subject do you like? Why?
4. What do you do after school?
5. What time do you get up on Saturdays?
6. What do you do on Saturday afternoons?

4 **Now watch the video and talk about your answers.**

They are the winners!

1 🔊49 **Look, listen and point. Who is happy at the end of the game?**

2 🔊50 **Write the numbers. Listen, check and say.**

golf	3		
score	☐	team	☐
flag	☐	prize	☐
volleyball	☐	hole	☐

3 Write the words from exercise 1.

1 You get a RIPEZ ____________ when you come first in a competition.

2 ELYLBLAVOL ____________ is a sport that two EMATS ____________ play.
When we play this, we hit the ball in the air with our hands or arms.
We don't want the ball to fall on the ground.

3 I played FOLG ____________ yesterday and hit the ball.
It hit the GLAF ____________ and went in the EOLH ____________.

4 51 **Find and write. Then listen and check. Say the words.**

snowball • sledge • snowboard • race
snowman • ~~skis~~

Look & Learn

snowboard	go snowboarding
sledge	go sledging
ski	go skiing

1 skis________ 2 ________ 3 ________

4 ________ 5 ________ 6 ________

5 52 **Read and complete. Then listen and check.**

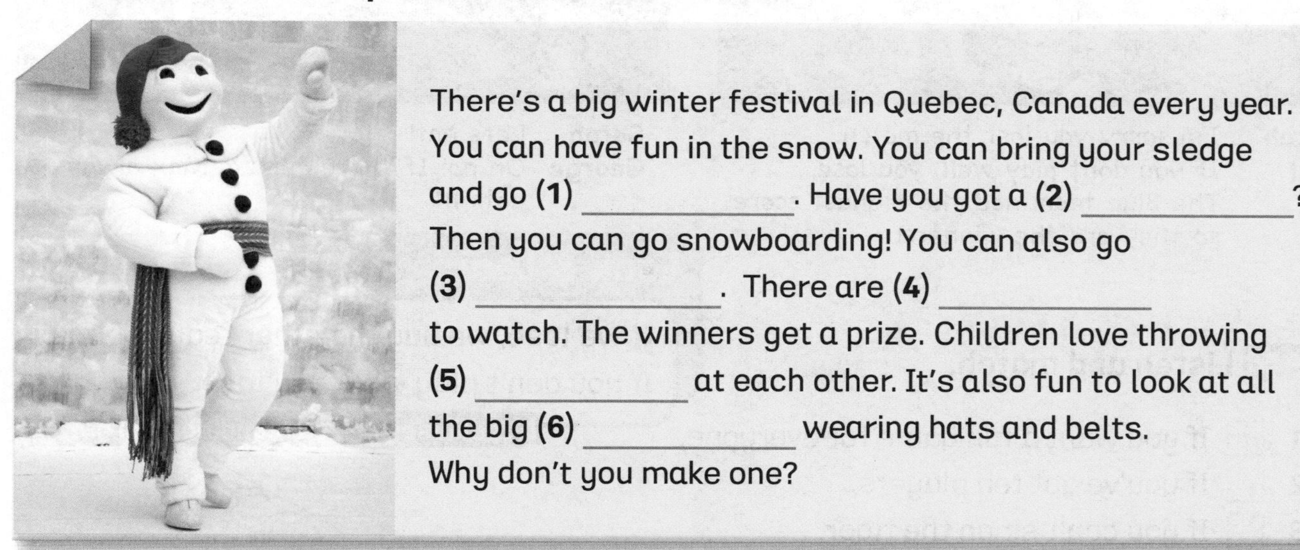

There's a big winter festival in Quebec, Canada every year. You can have fun in the snow. You can bring your sledge and go (**1**) ________. Have you got a (**2**) ________? Then you can go snowboarding! You can also go (**3**) ________. There are (**4**) ________ to watch. The winners get a prize. Children love throwing (**5**) ________ at each other. It's also fun to look at all the big (**6**) ________ wearing hats and belts. Why don't you make one?

6 53 Say the Sounds **Listen and say these three times.**

It's not hot.
My snowman's cold.
There's a lot of snow!

7 Say & Play **Choose a card and mime.**

Are you throwing a snowball?

Yes, I am!

6 They are the winners!

8 54 Listen and read. What do they do after the match?

Sarah What do you do after a match?
Boy We all have pizzas together!

Boy If we lose, we buy the other team a pizza.
Girl But today the Blues were the winners, so they don't have to buy the pizzas.

Sarah I'm sorry you lost the match.
Girl If you don't play well, you lose. The Blue team had the highest score so they are the winners!

Sarah Let's eat!
George Oh no! If there's pizza, Max always eats it!

Look & Learn

If we lose, we buy the other team a pizza.
If you don't play well, you lose.

▶ *If* clauses (in zero conditionals) p. 139

9 55 Listen and match.

1 ☐ If you want a fun game for everyone,
2 ☐ If you've got ten players,
3 ☐ If you can't sit on the floor,
4 ☐ If the ball doesn't go over the net,
5 ☐ If your team hits the ball back over the net,

a your team scores.
b your team doesn't score.
c play this game!
d play in two teams of five, Team A and B.
e sit on chairs and hit the ball over the net.

10 Say & Play Match the cards to make sentences.

11 🔊56 Look and complete. Then listen and check.

~~fast enough~~ • too short • tall enough • too slow

Look & Learn

I didn't run **fast enough** = I was **too slow**.
I'm **too short** = I'm **not tall enough**.

Mum How was sports day today? Did you win any races?
Jack No, I didn't. I didn't run fast enough.
Mum You didn't win because you were (1) ___________?
Jack Yes.
Mum Did you play basketball?
Jack No! I wanted to play but I'm not (2) ___________!
Mum You're (3) ___________?
Jack Yes, I am.

12 Read and write. Use *too* or *enough*.

A Let's go for a walk.
B No, thanks. It's too cold to go for a walk.

1 **A** Can you help me carry this box?
B No, sorry. I'm not strong ___________.

2 **A** Do you want to go to the cinema tonight?
B I can't. I'm ___________ busy with my homework.

3 **A** Can you open that window, please?
B No, sorry. I'm not tall ___________.

4 **A** Can I go on that scary ride at the funfair, please?
B No, you can't. You're ___________ young.

13 Say & Play Student A, look at the sentence beginnings and endings below. Student B, look at page 126. Take turns and finish the sentences.

Student A

Beginnings	Endings
We can't go swimming	because it's too dark.
We can't fly our kites	because it was too long.
I can't climb that tree	because I'm too ill.
I can't hear the music	because I stayed up too late last night.
I couldn't sleep last night	because it was too expensive.
I can't ride a motorbike	because they're too small.

6 FLYERS PRACTICE

Listening Part 4

1 57 **Listen and tick (✔) the box. There is one example.**

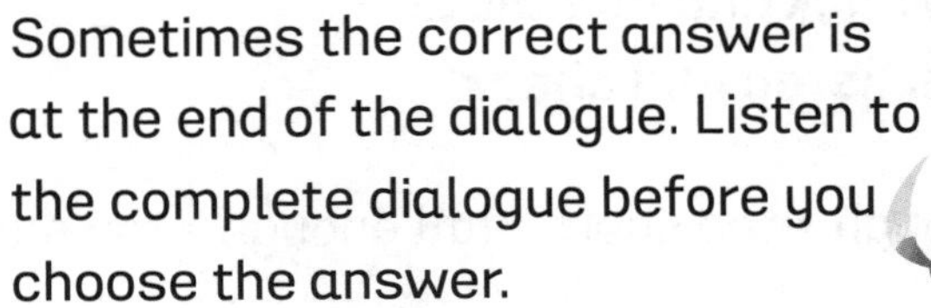

What's Katy's favourite sport?

A  ✔
B 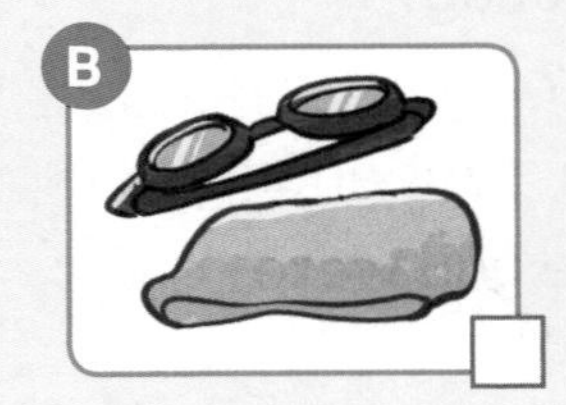
C 

1 What does Katy do if it rains on holiday?

A 
B 
C 

2 What did Katy lose on holiday?

A 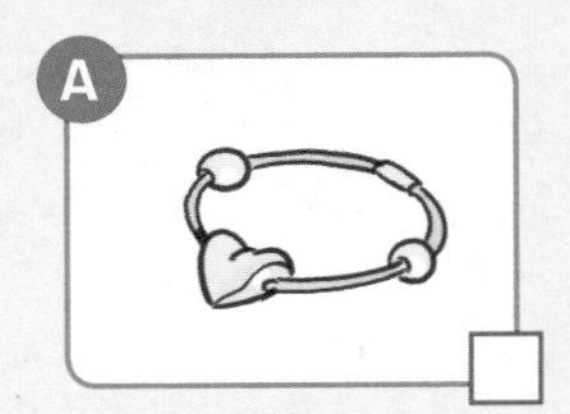
B 
C 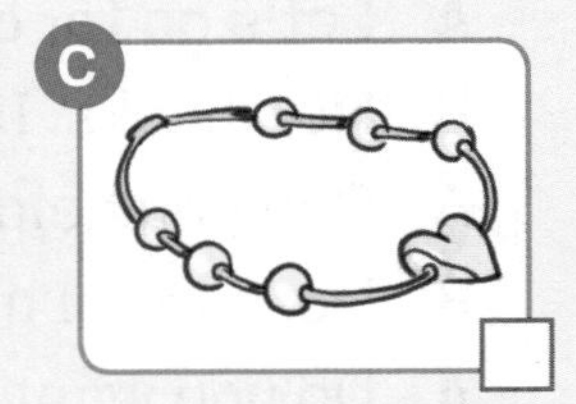

3 What do Katy and her brother like doing in the park?

A 
B 
C 

4 What prize did Katy's brother win?

A 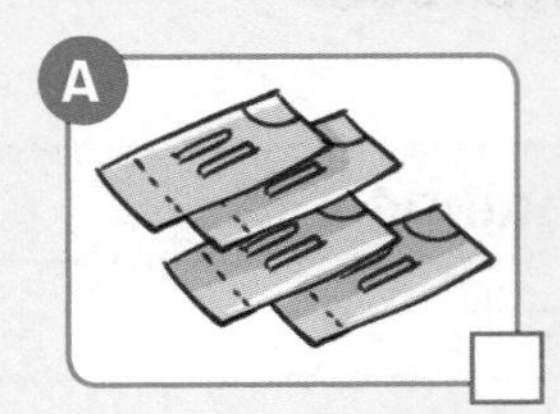
B 
C 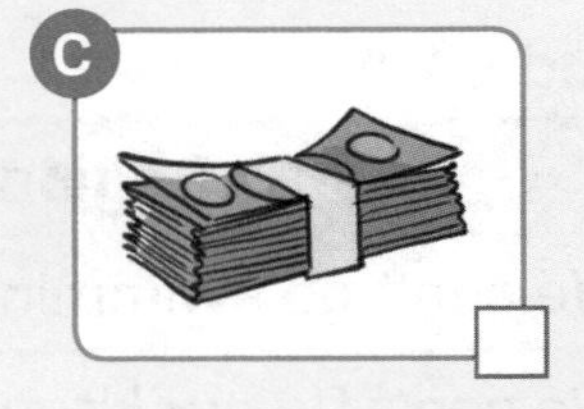

5 What did Katy eat at the restaurant?

A 
B 
C 

Reading and Writing Part 7

2 **Look at the three pictures. Write about this story. Write 20 or more words.**

Look carefully at all three pictures before you start writing. Write one or two sentences about each picture first, then try to put them together to make a story.

____

____

____

____

7 He plays the drums

1 58 **Listen and find the words. What is the name of the band?**

2 59 **Write the numbers. Listen, check and say.**

concert	1	singer		instruments	
pop music		tune		rock music	
drums		noisy		violin	

3 Read and complete.

rock • ~~instruments~~ • concert • singer • tunes

In music class you learn to play different instruments.

1 I can play ____________ on the piano.
2 I've got two tickets to a pop ____________.
3 Do you like ____________ music?
4 Who is the ____________ in the band?

4 🔊60 Read and match. Then listen and check. Say the words in blue.

1 ☐ I love doing **puzzles**.

2 ☐ My hobby is playing **chess**.

3 ☐ I **make models**.

4 ☐ I **collect** stamps.

5 ☐ I **draw cartoons**.

6 ☐ I read **magazines**.

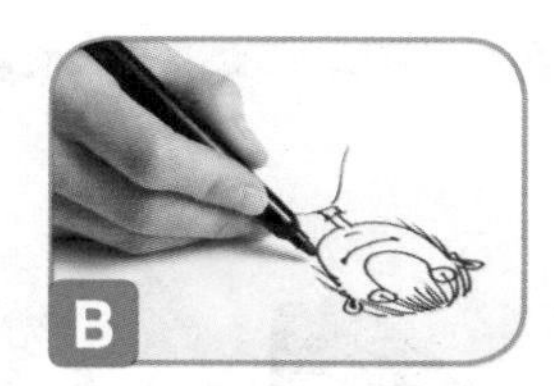

5 🔊61 Read and complete. Then listen and check.

Come to our Hobby club!

Every Friday after school.

✔ We've got lots of __________ and comics to read.
✔ If you like comics, learn to __________ __________ and make your own comics!
✔ You can play video games, board games or __________.
✔ Do you like doing __________? You can do this alone or with a friend!
✔ We can help you __________ __________ from paper, card, metal, wool or wood.
✔ Come and see the things some of the students __________ – stamps, baseball caps and football T-shirts!

6 Say & Play What's my hobby? Look and ask questions.

7 He plays the drums

7 62 Listen and read. What instrument does Ben play?

Sarah Hey, this is your brother's band, isn't it?
George Yes, the Rock Rabbits. They've got a concert at school tonight.
Sarah Ben plays the guitar well, doesn't he?
George Yes, he does. Let's go to the concert.

Sarah Hi, Ben! What's wrong? Why isn't your band playing?
Ben We can't play. The boy who plays the drums is ill.
George I can play the drums for you!
Ben You can't play the drums!
George Yes, I can. Just watch!

Sarah George! What are you talking about? You can't really play the drums, can you?
George Don't worry! I can learn!

Emma He isn't very good, is he?
Sarah No, he can't play the drums at all! But he's very funny, isn't he?

8 63 Say the Sounds Listen and say.

Ben plays the guitar well, doesn't he? ↘

You can't play the drums, can you? ↗

Look & Learn

This **is** your brother's band, **isn't** it?
He **isn't** very good, **is** he?

▶ Tag questions p. 139

9 64 Read and match. Then listen, check and say.

1 ☐ This is a nice tune,
2 ☐ It isn't very nice,
3 ☐ You don't like rock music,
4 ☐ You've got a lot of unusual stamps,
5 ☐ Those bottles are empty,

a is it?
b haven't you?
c aren't they?
d isn't it?
e do you?

Look & Learn

She **likes** doing puzzles.

I'm **interested in** golf.

I like pop music, but
I **prefer** rock music.
✔ pop ✔✔ rock

I **don't mind** playing chess.

I'm **not interested in** football.

He **doesn't like** golf.

10 65 Circle the correct words. Listen and check.

Ann Do you like playing video games?
Rob Yes, but I **(1) prefer / don't like** playing chess.
Ann Really? You like playing chess more than playing video games?
Rob Yes! I **(2) don't mind / don't like** playing video games, but playing chess is my favourite. **(3) Do you like / Are you interested in** learning to play chess? I can teach you.
Ann Not now! There's a football match on TV. Do you want to watch that first?
Rob No, thanks. **(4) I'm not interested in / I don't mind** football.

11 Read and complete.

1 **A** Do you want to go to a **tennis match** with me?
B No, thanks. I'm not ____________ in **tennis**.
2 **A** Which do you like best – **pop music** or **rock music**?
B I like rock music, but I ____________ pop music.
3 **A** Which do you prefer – **board games** or **puzzles**?
B I ____________ ____________. I like both.

12 Say & Play Change the words in blue in exercise 11 and talk with a friend.

FLYERS PRACTICE

Listening Part 5

1 66 **Listen and colour and write. There is one example.**

Listen to the instructions carefully. You have to write two words in the places you are told to.

Reading and Writing Part 1

2 Look and read. Choose the correct words and write them on the lines. There is one example.

Read all the words before you answer the questions.

a model | chess | golf | volleyball | a comic | a drum | a dictionary | a violin | magazines | a band | a letter | stamps | a puzzle | winner | a prize

You can use metal, wood or paper to make this. a model

1 It's a game for two players. You play it on a board with black and white squares. ____________

2 It's an instrument that you hit to make a sound. ____________

3 You get this when you win a competition or come first in a race. ____________

4 This is the person who comes first in a race or a competition. ____________

5 You put these on an envelope before you post it. Some people collect them. ____________

6 People don't usually play this game in teams. They hit a small, hard white ball into a hole. ____________

7 This is a group of people playing instruments together. ____________

8 This instrument is made of wood. It's smaller than a guitar. ____________

9 You play this sport in a team of six players. You can play inside or outside. ____________

10 You use this book to find out what a word means. ____________

8 Can you move your toes?

1 🔊67 **Look, listen and point. Who goes in the ambulance?**

2 🔊68 **Write the numbers. Listen, check and say.**

ambulance	3	elbow	☐	x-ray	☐
toes	☐	fingers	☐	medicine	☐
knee	☐	bandage	☐	broken	☐

3 🔊69 **Write the words. Listen and check.**

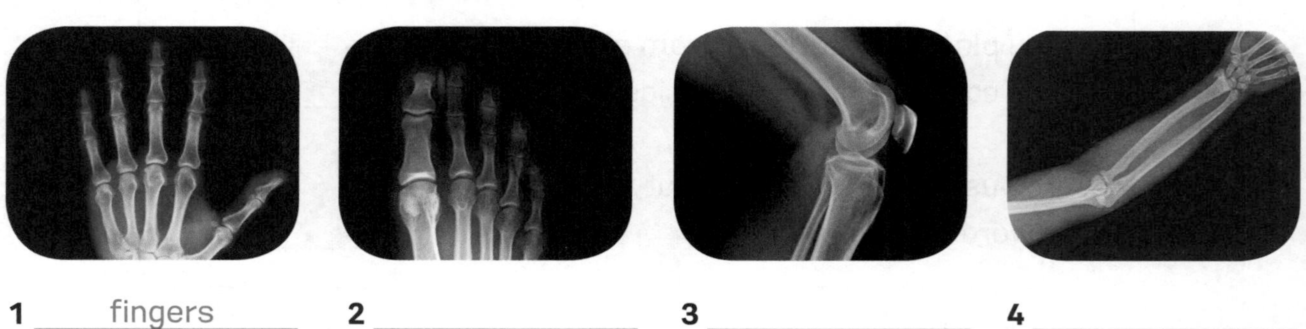

1 ___fingers___ 2 ____________ 3 ____________ 4 ____________

4 🔊70 Find and write. Then listen and check. Say the words.

burn your hand • have a sore toe • ~~cut your finger~~ • break your arm • fall over

1 cut your finger
2 ______
3 ______
4 ______
5 ______

Look & Learn

present	past
break	broke
cut	cut
burn	burnt/burned
hurt	hurt
fall over	fell over

5 🔊71 Listen and draw lines. Then write.

Emma	make cup of tea	cut knee and elbow
William	walk into a door	break arm
May	fall over	hurt head
Jack	fall over	burn hand

Emma fell over and cut her knee and elbow.
1 William ______
2 May ______
3 Jack ______

6 Say & Play Choose a word from each group. Act and guess.

8 Can you move your toes?

7 72 **Listen and read. Why can't Ben go roller skating?**

Doctor Your elbow is OK, Ben, but you should wear this bandage for a few days.
Ben OK. What about my knee?

Doctor Your knee is OK, but this little toe is broken. Look at the x-ray.
Ben Yes, that toe is sore. What should I do?
Doctor You should take this medicine in the morning and evening.

Ben Can I go roller skating soon?
Doctor No, you can't. You shouldn't go roller skating or play football for six weeks.
Ben Oh, no!

Ben I can't play football for six weeks.
George You're lucky. You don't have to go to school.
Mum Er, no! You should take your medicine, go to bed early and go to school.

8 **Read the story again and write *should* or *shouldn't*.**

1 Ben ____________ wear the bandage.
2 He ____________ take medicine.
3 He ____________ play football.
4 He ____________ run.
5 He ____________ go to bed early.
6 He ____________ go to school.

Look & Learn

What **should** I do?
You **should take** this medicine.
You **shouldn't play** football.

Should I **wear** the bandage at home?
Yes, you **should**.

▶ *should* p. 139

9 73 **Read and circle. Listen and check.**

WHAT SHOULD YOU DO?

FIRST AID

1 You burn your hand on the oven.
Should you
A hold your hand under cold water?
B put your hand under hot water?
C put a bandage on your hand?

2 You drop a dictionary on your foot and hurt your toe. Should you
A call an ambulance?
B drop a book on the other foot?
C take off your shoe and put your sore foot on a chair?

3 You cut your finger with a knife.
Should you first
A put a bandage on it?
B clean your finger in cold water?
C put some medicine on it?

4 Your friend can't stop coughing.
Should you
A hit their back four or five times?
B drink some water?
C tell them to be quiet?

5 Your friend is riding a horse.
She falls and breaks her arm. She
A should move her arm.
B shouldn't move her arm.
C should get back on her horse.

6 Your friend is riding his bike. He falls and hurts his head. Should he
A ride his bike home?
B put a bandage on it?
C hold something cold on his head?

7 Remember! If you need help, you **should / shouldn't** tell a parent or a grown-up.

10 74 Say the Sounds **Listen and say this three times.**

You shouldn't sit in the sun.

11 Say & Play **Student A, look at the card below. Student B, look at the card on page 127. Talk with a friend.**

Student A

Ask what's wrong	What's the matter, (*name*)?
Ask what happened	What happened? / How did you do it?
Respond and give advice	Oh no! / Oh dear. You should / shouldn't... run / go to school / take some medicine / go to bed / go to the doctor's / wear a bandage

8 FLYERS PRACTICE

Speaking Part 2

1 75 **Ask questions to find the missing information. Student A look at this page, Student B look at page 127.**

Use the information to make sentences when you answer the questions.

Student A

William's Sunday

Where	?
What / happen	?
How	?
Mum or Dad help	?
Call ambulance	?

Helen's Sunday

Where	in the garden at home
What / happen	broke leg
How	fell over
Mum or Dad help	Dad
Call ambulance	yes

Speaking Part 4

2 Ask and answer the questions with your partner.

1. What's your favourite sport?
2. What do you like doing in the winter?
3. What are your favourite hobbies?
4. Which games do you like?
5. What kind of music do you prefer – pop music or rock music?
6. I fell over in the playground and hurt my leg. What should I do?

3 **Now watch the video and talk about your answers.**

Reading and Writing Part 6

4 Read the diary and write the missing words. Write one word on each line.

Read the text to the end before you write any words.

I'm not enjoying my holiday! This morning we walked a long way.

Example My boots are too small so my ___toes___ are sore now. In the afternoon

1 we played football and I fell ______________ and hurt my elbow. In the

evening we cooked burgers outside. First, we had to find some wood and

make a fire. The teacher said, 'Be careful!' but Harry touched the

2 hot wood and ______________ his hand. Harry wanted us to call an

3 ______________ and go to hospital, but the teacher said 'You don't need to

4 go to hospital. You ______________ hold it under some cold water.' Harry

5 cried ______________ it was really sore.

When Harry felt better, we sat together and ate the burgers.

REVISION 5-8

1 Find the words.

Across

3 In this sport you hit a small hard ball into a hole.
5 You travel to hospital in this.
6 You use this to find words in different languages.
10 You learn about the world in this subject at school.

Down

1 You get this if you win a competition.
2 You do this sport in the snow.
7 A board game with black and white squares.
4 You wear this if you hurt your arm.
8 We have lunch at ______.
9 It's between your shoulder and your hand.

2 Complete the story.

toe • magazine • cartoons • stamps • volleyball • midnight • drums

Richard wanted a new hobby. He liked sports, so he tried **(1)** ______, but he fell over and broke his **(2)** ______. He liked rock music so he tried playing the **(3)** ______ in a band. He practised for a concert until **(4)** ______ every night at home, but it was too noisy. 'How about playing chess or collecting **(5)** ______?' said his mum but Richard liked being in a team. He didn't want to be alone. 'Come and help us,' said his friend, Sophie. 'We're writing a school **(6)** ______'. Richard wrote about volleyball and rock music and he drew **(7)** ______ for the magazine. He was good at art. 'This is a great hobby', he said. 'I can do all of my favourite things!'

3 Watch the video. Then answer the questions.

1 What time does school start?
2 What do they do if it's sunny?
3 What did they do in the park last year?
4 What happened to Sarah?
5 What did the doctor say?
6 Does Sarah like art?

4 Write about you.

1 School starts at ____________________.
2 It finishes ____________________.
3 If it's sunny we ____________________ after school.
4 I'm interested in ____________________.
5 I like ____________________, but I prefer ____________________.
6 My teacher says I should ____________________.

5 Say & Play Tell the story. Take turns to say a sentence.

It was a sunny day.

William, Oliver and Sophia went to the park.

A DAY IN THE PARK

9 A storm at night

1 76 **Look, listen and point. What does Sammy want to do tonight?**

2 77 **Write the numbers. Listen, check and say.**

light	4	dark	☐
storm	☐	summer	☐
tent	☐	autumn	☐
warm	☐	winter	☐
foggy	☐	spring	☐

autumn (UK)
fall (US)

3 78 **Write the words. Listen and check.**

It's usually hot and sunny in summer.

1. It's cold and it snows in _________.
2. It's warm and the flowers grow in _________.
3. It's sometimes foggy and the leaves are orange in _________.
4. There's a lot of wind and rain when there's a _________.
5. You can sleep outside in a _________.

4 79 Find and write. Then listen and check. Say the words.

airport • ~~camp~~ • hotel • money • taxi • suitcase

In the summer holidays, we usually take our rucksacks and a tent and we camp in a field near our house. It's great fun! Last year was different. We spent a lot of (1) ________. We took a (2) ________ to the (3) ________ and flew to an island. When we arrived, Dad's (4) ________ was missing. He wasn't very happy. We stayed in a (5) ________. On the first night, there was a storm and the rain came into our room. I think I prefer our tent!

5 80 Listen and tick (✓).

1 Where do Jill and her family usually stay in winter?

A 
B 
C 

2 What's the weather like in the mornings?

A 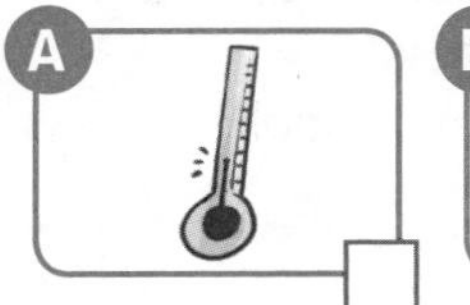
B 
C 

3 How do they get there?

A 
B 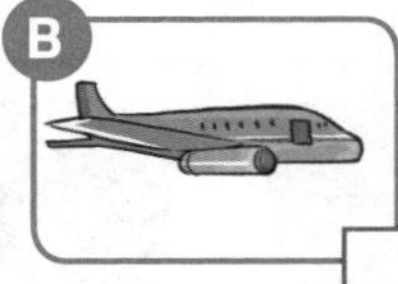
C 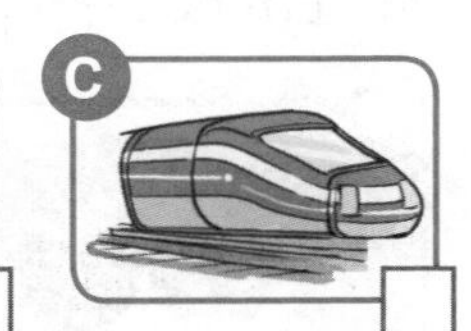

4 What's Jill's favourite season?

A 
B 
C 

6 Say & Play Cut out and play.

It's warm and sunny. I'm riding my bike in the park.

Yes!

Is it spring?

9 A storm at night

7 81 Listen and read. Why was Sarah frightened?

George What are you doing with that suitcase, Sarah?
Sarah Sammy and I are going to sleep in the tree house tonight!

Sarah We're going to read some stories, then we're going to go to sleep.
George Really? But it's winter and it's going to rain.
Sarah It's OK. It's warm in the tree house and I'm not frightened of storms.

Sarah ... and that's the end of the story. Sammy! What's that noise? I'm not going to go to sleep now!
Sammy I don't know. I'm going to look.

Sammy Ha, ha! It's Max. Were you frightened?
Sarah Ha, ha! Yes, I was.

Look & Learn

We**'re going to sleep** in the tree house.
I**'m not going to sleep** now.

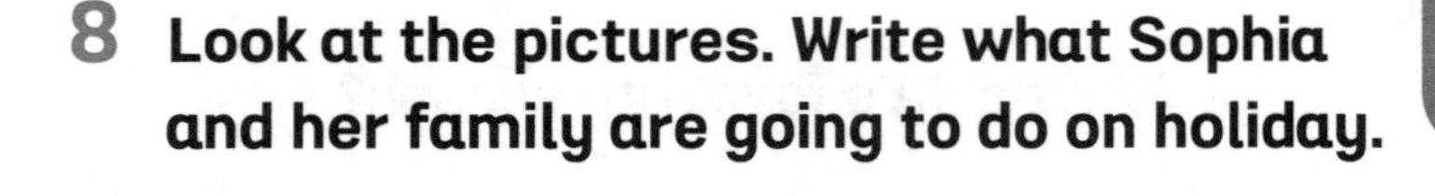

8 Look at the pictures. Write what Sophia and her family are going to do on holiday.

They 're going to sleep (sleep) in a hotel.
They aren't going to sleep (sleep) in a tent.
1 It ________________ (be) hot and sunny.
2 It ________________ (be) cold and foggy.
3 She ________________ (swim) in the sea.
4 She ________________ (go) to school.

9 82 Choose and write. Listen and check.

going to • ~~camp~~ • be • not going to • take • are

Look & Learn

What **are** you **going to do**?
Where **are** you **going to go**?

Robert What are you going to do in the summer holidays, Holly?
Holly We're going to ___camp___ in our tent.
Robert Where are you going to go?
Holly We're (**1**) ________ go to the mountains.
Robert What's the weather going to be like?
Holly It's going to (**2**) ________ warm and sunny.
Robert What (**3**) ________ you going to take?
Holly We're going to (**4**) ________ our tent, blankets, food, walking boots, swimsuits ...
Robert Have you got a big suitcase?
Holly I'm (**5**) ________ take a suitcase, Robert! I'm going to take a rucksack – a very big rucksack!

10 Write questions about the summer holidays.

What / do? ___What are you going to do?___
1 When / go? ________
2 Who / go with? ________
3 Where / stay? ________
4 What / weather / be like? ________
5 What / you / take? ________
6 What / you / eat? ________
7 What / you / play? ________

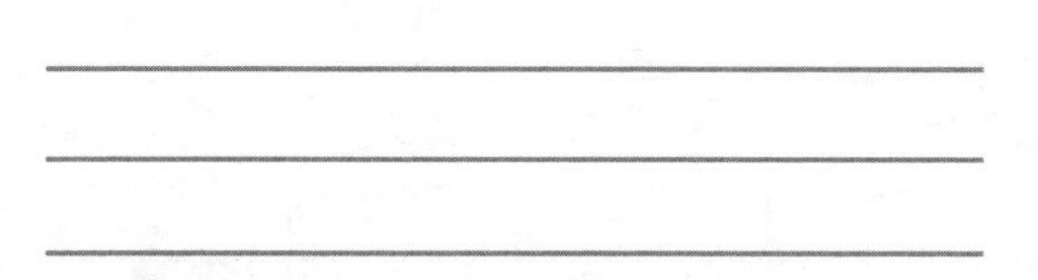

11 Say & Play Cut out and play.

Where are you going to go?

I'm going to go to the moon.

What are you going to do?

I'm going to camp in a tent. I'm not going to swim with a dolphin.

FLYERS PRACTICE

Speaking Part 1

1 🔊83 **Look at the pictures. Find six differences.**

Look carefully at the shape and size of things in the picture and where they are.

2 ▶ **Now watch the video and talk about your answers.**

Reading and Writing Part 5

3 **Look at the picture and read the story. Write some words to complete the sentences about the story. You can use 1, 2, 3 or 4 words.**

PAUL AND HIS FRIEND CAMP IN THE COUNTRYSIDE

Last spring, Paul went away with his friend Oliver and Oliver's dad. Oliver had a new tent and he wanted to camp in the countryside. They drove a long way and stopped at a farm. 'We can camp in that field near the river,' said Oliver's dad. The weather was warm and sunny and Oliver and Paul had a great afternoon. They played football and swam in the river. In the evening, they were hungry so they made a fire and cooked sausages. They played games until it was dark, then they went to bed in the new tent. They were really tired. In the night, there was a lot of wind and rain.

Paul woke up early the next morning. He got up and looked outside. There was water everywhere after the storm. 'Wake up!' he shouted. Oliver and his dad got up quickly and they carried their wet things to the car. 'Let's stay in a hotel in the town tonight,' said Oliver's dad. So they went to a hotel. Oliver's dad said it was expensive, but they were happy to be warm and dry.

Next year, Oliver wants Paul to camp with him again, but they learnt a lesson. They're going to go in summer when it is dry.

Examples

Oliver and his dad took Paul on holiday last spring.

They camped on a farm in Oliver's new tent.

Questions

1 In the afternoon, the boys had fun in ______________.

2 For dinner, they ______________ which they cooked over a fire.

3 They ______________ before they went to bed.

4 During the night, there was ______________.

5 In the morning, their things ______________.

6 They slept ______________ the next night.

7 Next year, they aren't going to camp in ______________.

What a cool car!

1 84 **Look, listen and point. Where are the people going by train?**

2 85 **Write the numbers. Listen, check and say.**

racing car [2]
fire engine [ ]
passengers [ ]
wheel [ ]
platform [ ]
railway [ ]
rocket [ ]
bicycle [ ]

fire engine (UK)
fire truck (US)

3 86 **Write the words. Listen and check.**

1 They've got wheels. ____________ ____________ ____________
2 It goes to the moon. ____________
3 They're at the railway station. ____________ ____________

4 87 Find and write. Then listen and check. Say the words.

lift • tyres • cycle • ~~push~~ • traffic • motorway • repair

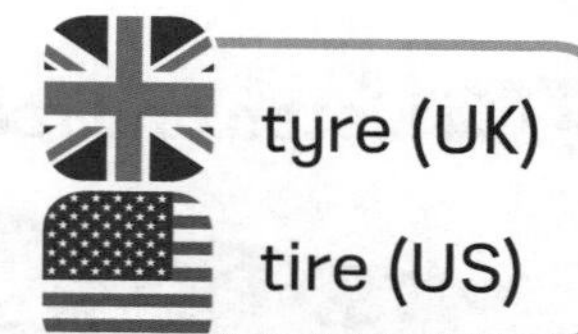

1 push 2 ________ 3 ________ 4 ________ 5 ________ 6 ________ 7 ________

5 88 Say the Sounds Listen and say.

I wear an orange jacket. I'm not a passenger.
I drive a red fire engine. It's a dangerous job.

6 Read and complete.

push • passengers • ~~cycle~~ • lift • railway • motorway • traffic • platform • bicycle

Charlie

I often (1) cycle to school. My school is at the top of a hill and I have to (2) ________ my (3) ________ up the hill. If it's raining, my mum gives me a (4) ________ in her car.

I use the (5) ________ to go to school. I walk to the station and meet my friends on the (6) ________. Sometimes there are lots of (7) ________ and we can't get on the train.

Lily

Paul

My dad takes me school. We go on the (8) ________ because it's quicker but sometimes there's a lot of (9) ________ and it's slow.

7 Say & Play Choose a card and describe the word. How quickly can your friend guess the word?

It's big and red and has more than two wheels. It carries a lot of water. It can be very noisy when you see it in the street.

It's a fire engine!

10 What a cool car!

8 89 Listen and read. What was wrong with the bicycle?

Dad My tyre! How did that happen? I was riding my bike yesterday and it was fine then.

Dad Ben, do you know what happened to my tyre?
Ben No, Dad. I wasn't home this morning. I was practising with the band. Does George know what happened?

Dad Hi, George! Were you in the tree house this morning?
George Yes, I was.
Dad What were you doing?
George I was repairing a hole in the roof. Why? Oh! Sorry, Dad.

Sarah Hey, George. Did you repair the roof of the tree house?
George Yes, I did. Now I'm repairing the hole in my dad's tyre!

Look & Learn

I **was riding** my bike yesterday.
I **was practising** with the band all day.
What **were you doing**?

▶ Past continuous p. 140

9 Look and write. What were they doing at different times?

1 At 8:30 this morning, I / cycle / to school.
At 8:30 this morning, I was cycling to school.

2 At 12 o'clock, we / have / lunch.

____

3 At 4 o'clock, Katy / write / a story for her English homework.

____

4 At 5:30, lots of passengers / wait / on the platform.

____

5 At 6 o'clock, my mum / drive / home from work.

____

10 Choose and complete.

build • not do • practise • rain • prepare • repair • ~~work~~

Oliver didn't have a very good day yesterday.
He wanted to go out for a walk before lunch, but we were all busy. Mum usually takes him out but she wasn't at home. She was working in town.
Dad (1) ______________ the lunch so he couldn't go.
Harry and his friend (2) ______________ a model racing car for their school project. Clare (3) ______________ the piano – her piano exam is next week.
And I (4) ______________ my bicycle tyre.
At 4 o'clock, I (5) ______________ anything. But the weather was terrible then.
It (6) ______________ so poor Oliver didn't have a walk.

11 Say & Play Student A, look at the card below. Student B, look at the card on page 128. Talk with a friend and complete your card.

Student A

What was Jack doing yesterday at these times?

7.00 a.m.	get up
8.00 a.m.	______________
8.30 a.m.	cycle to school
11.00 a.m.	______________
3.30 p.m.	walk home
5.00 p.m.	______________
6.30 p.m.	do homework
10.00 p.m.	______________

What was Jack doing yesterday at 8 o'clock in the morning?

He was having breakfast.

FLYERS PRACTICE

Speaking Part 3

1 90 **Listen. Then continue to tell the story.**

You only have to say a few words about each picture, but you must talk about all the pictures.

JIM GOES TO SCHOOL

2 **Now watch the video and talk about your answers.**

Reading and Writing Part 3

3 Read the story. Choose a word from the box. Write the correct word next to numbers 1-5. There is one example.

Read the story to the end before you choose the missing words.

example

ride	passengers	lift	repaired	traffic
cycled	arrived	came	motorway	railway

Jill woke up and saw that it was raining. 'I can't ___ride___ my bike to school in the rain,' she said to her mum. 'I can give you a **(1)** ___________. I can drive past the school on my way to work.' Jill got ready for school, and she and her mum got in the car. 'Let's go on the **(2)** ___________,' said Mum. 'It's quicker.' But there was so much **(3)** ___________! The cars were moving very slowly. So, at the railway station, Jill's mum said, 'I think you should get the train from here. I don't want you to be late for school.' Jill bought a ticket and went onto the platform. There were a lot of **(4)** ___________ there! They were all waiting for the same train. But the train was full and Jill couldn't get on. Finally, Jill **(5)** ___________ at school – late, and wet from the rain. But her teacher wasn't angry. She gave Jill a towel to dry her hair and said, 'I also got wet in the rain today!'

(6) Now choose the best name for the story. Tick one box.

A terrible journey to school ☐ Jill's teacher ☐ Mum drives to work ☐

What kind of animal is that?

1 🔊91 **Look, listen and point. How many birds are there?**

2 🔊92 **Write the numbers. Listen, check and say.**

dinosaur	1	beetle	☐	butterfly	☐
eagle	☐	swan	☐	fur	☐
octopus	☐	camel	☐	tortoise	☐

3 **Look and write.**

They walk on land.	They live in the sea.	They can fly.
a beetle, ________	________	________
________	________	________
________	________	________
________	________	________

4 🔊93 Find and write. Then listen and check. Say the words.

insect • wings • nest • furry • extinct • wild

1 A kitten is soft and ________________.
2 A swan builds its ________________ next to a river.
3 Dinosaurs are ________________. They lived millions of years ago.
4 Elephants and polar bears are ________________ animals.
5 An eagle has two enormous ________________.
6 A beetle is an ________________.

5 Read and choose.

1 Which animal makes a nest?
A ☐ an eagle B ☐ a camel C ☐ an octopus

2 Which two creatures have wings?
A ☐ a swan B ☐ a tortoise C ☐ a butterfly

3 Which of these is an insect?
A ☐ an eagle B ☐ a butterfly C ☐ a swan

4 Which animal is furry?
A ☐ a polar bear B ☐ an octopus C ☐ a tortoise

6 Say & Play Pick up a card and describe the creature. Can your friend guess the word?

It's an insect. It's got four beautiful wings.

It's a butterfly!

What kind of animal is that?

7 🔊94 Listen and read. What is Bill afraid of?

Sarah Hello, Bill Strong. I love your books! Have you ever ridden a camel?
Bill Yes, I have!

George Have you ever swum with dolphins?
Bill No, I haven't.
George My brother has swum with dolphins!
Bill Really? He's very lucky!

Sarah Have you ever been to a jungle?
Bill Yes, I have.
Sarah That's amazing! I love wild animals.

Sarah Have you ever seen a very big spider?
Bill No, I ... Yes, I have! Aargh! I'm afraid of spiders!

8 Write questions and complete the answers.

you ever / climb / a mountain?
Have you ever climbed a mountain?
Yes, I have.

Look & Learn

ride – rode – ridden
Have you **ever ridden** a camel?
Yes, I **have**. No, I **haven't**.
swim – swam – swum
My brother **has** / **hasn't swum** with dolphins.

1 you ever / ride / an elephant?
______________________ No, I ______________.

2 your ever / hold / a snake?
______________________ Yes, I ______________.

3 you ever / see / an eagle?
______________________ No, I ______________.

4 your parents ever / sleep / in a tent?
______________________ No, they ______________.

5 your friend ever / swim / in a river?
______________________ Yes, he ______________.

9 Read. Then write sentences about the things they have or have never done.

Today we are talking to Betty Brave! She's written a book about her adventures.

Have you been to lots of different places, Betty?
Yes, I've been all over the world. I've been to jungles and forests. I've swum in the sea and I've climbed mountains. But I've never visited this town! It's my first time here.
Thank you for coming! Tell us about the amazing animals you've seen on your adventures.
I've seen tigers, polar bears and lions. My husband and I have swum with whales, but we've never seen a shark!

Does your husband like adventures too?
Yes. We've been on lots of exciting journeys together. But he's never ridden an elephant in the jungle.
My children like adventures too, but they have never climbed a mountain.
And there's another adventure my husband and children have never had. They've never written a book!

Betty / travel all over the world.
Betty has travelled all over the world.

1 She / visit this town.
____

2 Her husband / swim with whales.
____

3 Betty and her husband / see a shark.
____

4 Betty's husband / ride an elephant.
____

5 Her children / have lots of adventures.
____

6 They / climb a mountain.
____

7 Betty's husband and children / write a book.
____

10 Say & Play Work in pairs. Write three sentences about things you have / have never done. Write two true sentences and one false sentence. Can your partner guess which sentence is true?

I've eaten snails.
I've never been to London.
I've never won a prize.

I think number one is false, and the others are true.

Yes, number one is false! I've never eaten snails.

11 FLYERS PRACTICE

Listening Part 1

1 95 **Listen and write. There is one example.**

Look at the picture before you listen and think about how to talk about each person and what they are doing.

Reading and Writing Part 4

2 Read the text. Choose the right words and write them on the lines.

For each question, there are three words to choose from. You don't have to think of a word yourself.

DINOSAURS

Example	There are so many different animals and birds ___in___ our world.
1	Millions of years ago, there ____________ dinosaurs, too,
2	____________ they are now extinct. These days, we only see them in
3	films and in books. We always think ____________ are very scary, but not
4	all dinosaurs were dangerous. Most of ____________ creatures were
5	enormous, but some were ____________ than a chicken.
6	Some had very long bodies and small heads. Most dinosaurs ____________ plants – like the one in the picture, but some preferred meat.
7	And did you know that there were dinosaurs ____________ had hair
8	on their bodies! Which other animals are ____________ to be
9	extinct ____________ the future? What do you think we can do
10	to save ____________?

Example	for	in	on
1	be	are	were
2	but	so	or
3	them	they	it
4	these	this	their
5	smallest	smaller	small
6	eat	eaten	ate
7	which	where	who
8	go	going	have
9	in	for	to
10	it	this	them

12 Our world

1 🔊96 **Look, listen and point. What does Sarah want to do?**

2 🔊97 **Write the numbers. Listen, check and say.**

Earth	7	desert	
planet		air	
fire		land	
ocean		space	

3 **Write the words.**

1 The sun and the moon are in ...
2 Our cities are built on ...
3 Animals and people need food, water and ...
4 When it's too hot in the forests, there are ...
5 There are eight ...
6 It doesn't rain often here.
7 Fish, dolphins and sharks live here.
8 The planet where we live.

1	2		3	4		5		6	7	8
e	n	v	i	r	o	n	m	e	n	t

4 98 Find and write. Then listen and check. Say the words.

bridge • wood • ~~pond~~ • stream • cave • hill • path

1 pond
2 ________
3 ________
4 ________
5 ________
6 ________
7 ________

5 99 Say the Sounds Listen and say. Then write the words.

I see a creature on the bridge. It's an eagle.
It's looking for fish in the stream.

see	bridge

6 100 Choose and write. Then listen and check.

What did you see in the stream? • Were there any bees? • we saw lots of insects • but we saw some ducks on the pond • ~~they weren't in the cave~~ • we went up the hill

Man What did you see on your walk?

Boy Well, we saw some bats but they weren't in the cave. They flew out! It was scary! Then we followed the path to the stream.

Man (1) ________________.

Boy We saw some fish and some frogs.

Man Did you see any insects?

Boy Yes, (2) ________________ on the ground and in the air. There were some black beetles on the bridge. There was one under a stone. Then (3) ________________ and had a picnic with some cows! We also saw some beautiful butterflies.

Man (4) ________________. Bees are important for the environment.

Boy Yes, after lunch we walked through the wood and saw some bees.

Man Oh good! What about birds? Did you see an eagle in the wood?

Boy No, we didn't, (5) ________________ on our way home. And we saw some nests in the trees.

Man What an interesting walk!

12 Our world

7 101 **Listen and read. How did George save water?**

George Happy Earth Day, Sarah! Have you saved the planet yet?
Sarah No, I haven't, but look, I've already started! I'm making a wild garden.

Sarah I've already fed the birds. I put some bread on the bird table this morning and the birds have already eaten it!
George Have you planted the flowers yet?
Sarah Yes, I've just planted them. Look at my dirty hands!

Sarah What have you done for Earth Day, George?
George Well, I've already saved water. I didn't have a shower this morning.
Sarah Ha, ha! You can come and help me now. I haven't made the pond yet.

Sarah Oh, no! What's Max doing?
George He's helping you! He's making a hole for your pond!
Sarah Ha, ha! You need a shower now, George!

8 Make sentences. Use *already*, *yet* and *just*.

Look & Learn

Have you **saved** the planet **yet**? No, I **haven't**.
I**'ve already fed** the birds.
I **haven't made** the pond **yet**.
I**'ve just planted** the flowers.

▶ Present perfect p. 140

feed the birds: Sarah has already fed the birds.

1 eat the food: The birds ____________.
2 plant the flowers: Sarah ____________.
3 have a shower: George ____________.
4 make a pond: They ____________.
5 make a hole: Max ____________.

9 Read the text. Then answer the questions.

AMAZING PLANET EARTH

Earth is the only planet where we can live. It has everything we need: food, water and air. Also, it's 150 million kilometres from the sun so it isn't too hot or too cold. Here are some facts about our special planet.

- The oceans are called the Atlantic, the Pacific, the Indian, the Arctic and the Southern Ocean.
- The Pacific is the largest and it's deeper than the other oceans. It's about four kilometres deep.
- There are a lot of rivers on Earth. The Amazon is longer than the other rivers. It's about 7,000 kilometres long.
- There are millions of lakes – about 117 million! Some are small and others are huge. The Caspian Sea is actually a lake.
- Everest is the highest mountain. Fourteen mountains are over 8000 metres high but Everest is about 9000 metres high.
- It's hot and sunny every day in the Sahara. It's one of the hottest deserts on Earth. It's also the largest!

kilometre (UK)
kilometer (US)

1 How far is the sun from the Earth? ______________
2 How many oceans are there? ______________
3 How deep is the deepest ocean? ______________
4 How long is the longest river? ______________
5 How many lakes are there? ______________
6 How high is the highest mountain? ______________
7 Which is the largest desert? ______________

Look & Learn

150 = a hundred and fifty
1,000 = a thousand
8,000 = eight thousand
1,000,000 = a million

10 Write the questions.

1 from / How far / the Earth? / is / the moon ______________
2 is / Which / ocean? / the smallest ______________
3 the highest / is / How high / waterfall? ______________
4 the biggest / lake? / is / Which ______________
5 cave? / How long / is / the longest ______________
6 How long / beach? / the longest / is ______________

11 Say & Play Student A look at this page. Student B, look at page 128.

Student A

The moon is 380,000 kilometres from the Earth.
The smallest ocean is ______________ .
The highest waterfall is about 1,000 metres high.
The biggest lake is ______________ .
The longest cave is ______________ long.
The longest beach is 212 kilometres long.

How far...?

12 FLYERS PRACTICE

Reading and Writing Part 5

1 Look at the picture and read the story. Write some words to complete the sentences about the story. You can use 1, 2, 3 or 4 words.

Be careful! You can't copy the words exactly from the story to complete the sentences.

TOM AND SALLY FIND A CAVE!

Tom and Sally were learning about the environment in geography. So last week, their geography teacher, Mrs Green, took them to the mountains. They went by bus and stopped near a wood.

Mrs Green gave everyone a map and said 'Follow the path, stay together and look for different animals. Then come back to the bus at half past three. It's a competition. The winner is the pair who finds the most animals.'

The children found beetles, butterflies and other insects in the wood. There was a stream where they saw fish and birds. At quarter past three Sally said, 'We have to go back now, Tom', but Tom said 'No! We haven't found enough animals yet and I can see a cave.' They went into the dark cave.

At half past three Mrs Green met the children at the bus, but Tom and Sally weren't there. The other children waited near the bus and counted the animals on their maps. Suddenly they heard a noise. It was Tom and Sally. Sally was shouting 'Help!' as they ran to the bus. 'Where have you been?' asked Mrs Green. 'What's wrong, Sally?' 'We found a cave ...' said Tom. 'We've just seen hundreds of bats,' said Sally. 'It was frightening.' 'Hundreds of bats?' asked Mrs Green. 'You've just won the competition! But you should listen to me next time.'

Examples

Mrs Green was teaching the children about the environment in geography.

Last week they went to a wood in the mountains.

Questions

1 They used ____________ to follow a path.

2 They walked in the wood and looked for ____________.

3 They went to a stream and found ____________.

4 Tom didn't want to go back because he saw ____________.

5 The children had to meet at the bus at ____________.

6 Sally was ____________ there were bats in the cave.

7 They won the competition because they saw ____________.

Listening Part 4

Look at each picture carefully before you listen. Then choose the best picture.

2 102 **Listen and tick (✓) the box. There is one example.**

What has Katy done today?

 B ☐ C ☐

1 Which insects has Katy seen?

2 What is Katy going to do next?

A ☐ B ☐ C ☐

3 Which books has Katy got?

4 What does Katy want to study?

 B ☐ C ☐

5 Where is Katy going to go this afternoon?

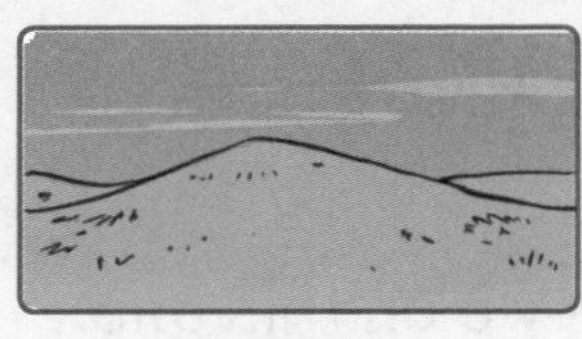  

 B ☐ C ☐

REVISION 9-12

1 Find one wrong word in lines 1-8. Choose the right words from the box.

cave • dinosaur • extinct • rocket • space • stream • ~~tents~~ • path • warm

Our teacher took us into the countryside for a weekend. We camped in a wood.

0	We slept in <u>nests</u>. The weather was lovely and	0	tents
1	dark. We went swimming in a nice, cool	1	______
2	desert. In the wood there was a big	2	______
3	hotel. I didn't want to explore it because that's where bats live!	3	______
	One night I heard a strange noise outside the tent. What was it?		
4	'Is it a butterfly?' I asked my friend.	4	______
5	'No! They're furry!' he laughed. 'They don't live on Earth anymore.'	5	______
6	'Perhaps a fire engine has come down from	6	______
7	airport!' I thought, 'with an alien in it.'	7	______
	We looked out but it was only our teacher.		
8	He was walking along the planet, looking up at the moon!	8	______

2 Read and complete the secret messages.

1. There are f ✱ v ● and the P ■ c ✱ f ✱ c is the biggest. They are all getting w ■ r m ● r.
   They are __ c __ __ ns.
2. You can c ■ r r y your clothes in this. Take it with you when you go on h ✱ l ✱ d ■ y.
   It's a s __ __ __ c __ __e.
3. It's always busy and n ✱ ✱ s y. There's a lot of t r ■ f f ✱ c.
   It's a m __ __ __ r __ __ y.

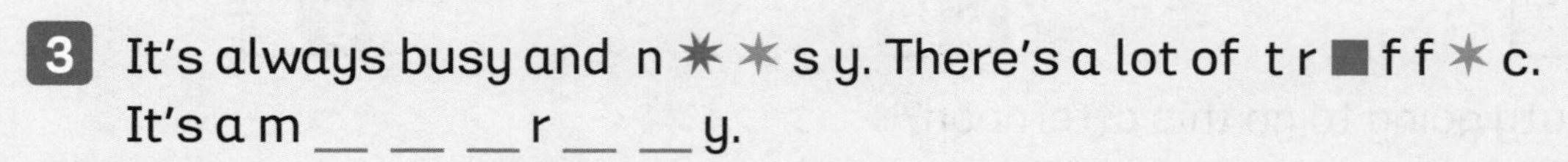

4. It's a small ✱ ns ● c t. It's got a hard s h ● l l and four w ✱ n g s
   It's a __ __ __ tle.
5. There are ● ✱ g h t p l ■ n ● t s in s p ● c e. We l ✱ v e on this one.
   __a __ t __

3 ▶ **Watch the video. Then answer the questions.**

It's the summer holidays!

1 Where is George now?
2 What season is it?
3 What has he just done?
4 What is he going to do tomorrow?
5 Has he ever seen a dolphin?
6 What hasn't he done yet?

4 Answer questions about you.

1 Where did you go on holiday last summer? ____________________
2 What did you do there? ____________________
3 What was the weather like yesterday? ____________________
4 What are you going to do tomorrow? ____________________
5 Have you ever seen any wild animals? ____________________

5 Say & Play **Look at the pictures. Find 8 differences.**

A

B

Places and directions

1 🔊103 **Look, listen and point. Who has a birthday soon?**

2 🔊104 **Write the numbers. Listen, check and say.**

castle	5	restaurant	
bank		theatre	
factory		chemist	
fire station		stadium	
police station		skyscraper	

theatre (UK)
theater (US)

3 🔊105 **Write the words. Listen and check.**

It's a huge old building. castle
1 We get medicine here. ________
2 It's a place where you have lunch or dinner. ________
3 Cars and other things are made here. ________
4 It's a very tall building. ________
5 It's a big place where there are sports matches and concerts. ________

4 106 Choose and write. Then listen and check. Say the words.

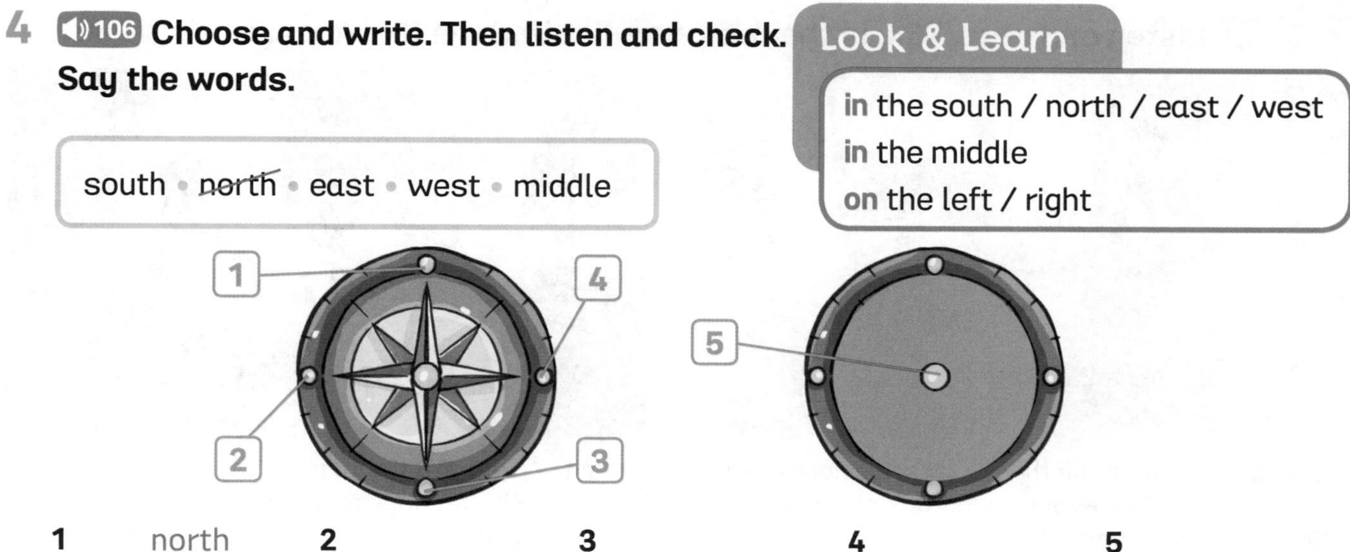

Look & Learn

in the south / north / east / west
in the middle
on the left / right

south • ~~north~~ • east • west • middle

1 north 2 ______ 3 ______ 4 ______ 5 ______

5 Read and find the places on Dolphin Island. Use words from exercise 2.

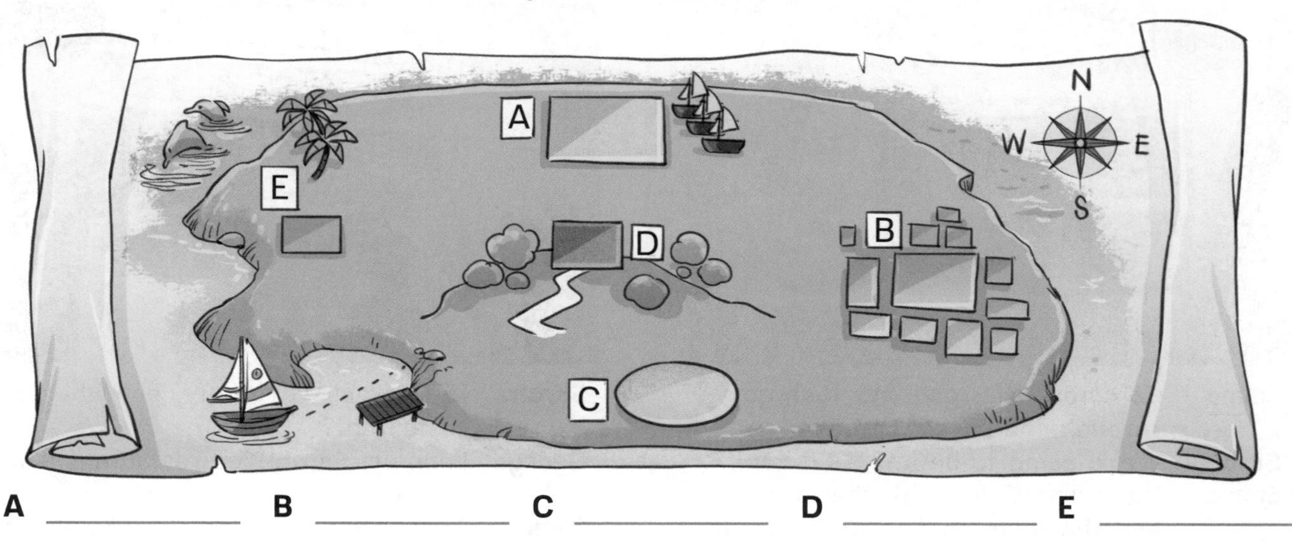

A ______ B ______ C ______ D ______ E ______

Visit Dolphin Island! The boat arrives in the south of the island. You can get a bus to the old castle on the hill in the middle of the island. The beaches are in the west. You can sometimes see dolphins from the beach. There are cafés and restaurants in the west too. If you want to go shopping, Dolphin Town is in the east of the island. There's a big theatre in the middle of the town. There's a bank and chemist too. There aren't any skyscrapers. In the north of the island there's a small factory where they make boats and surfboards. If you like sports, you can go to the stadium in the south of the island. There's a lot to see and do on Dolphin Island.

6 107 Say the Sounds. Listen and say.

There's a theatre in the south.
The weather is better in the north.

Places and directions

7 108 Listen and read. Why is the restaurant called the Sky Room?

George It's Ben's birthday dinner tomorrow at the Sky Room restaurant at seven o'clock.
Sarah OK. Where is it?
George It's in the middle of town, next to the park.

Emma I've got the map on my phone. Look.
Sarah OK, so go straight on and go over the bridge. Go past the bank on the left.
Emma OK. Let's go.

Emma Go across the road and then go through the park.
Sarah We're going to be late. Is it far?
Emma No, it isn't. Turn right, then turn left and the restaurant is on the right.

Sarah Hi George! We're here, but where's the restaurant?
George Look up, Sarah! The restaurant is on the roof.
Emma That's why it's called the Sky Room!

8 Look and complete.

Turn left

1 ________ the bank

2 ________ the road

3 ________ the bridge

4 ________

5 ________

6 ________ the park

Look & Learn

Turn **left**. / Turn **right**.
Go straight on.
Go over the bridge / **across** the road / **past** the school / **through** the park.
on the right / **on** the left

9 109 Listen and write the places on the map.

bank • theatre • castle

Look & Learn

Do you know the way to the bank?
Can you tell me the way to the theatre?
Where's the castle?

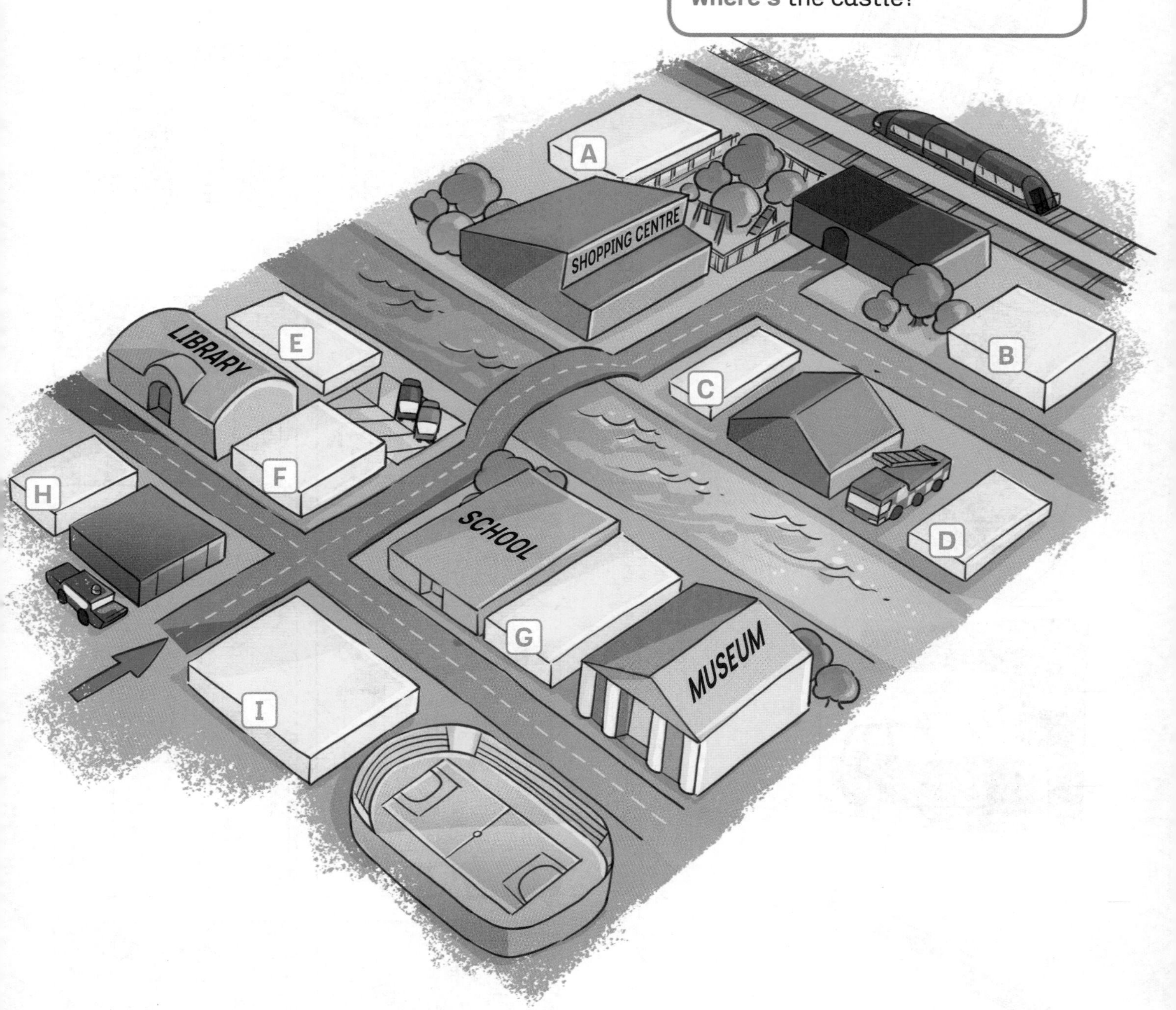

10 Say & Play Talk with a friend. Ask for directions to the cinema, post office, chemist or hospital.

Do you know the way to the cinema?

Go straight on ...

13 FLYERS PRACTICE

Listening Part 3

1 110 **Where did David get these things on his trip to London? Listen and write a letter in each box. There is one example.**

There are two pictures which are not correct. You don't need to use them all.

postcards [F]

map [ ]

chocolates [ ]

taxi [ ]

pen [ ]

rucksack [ ]

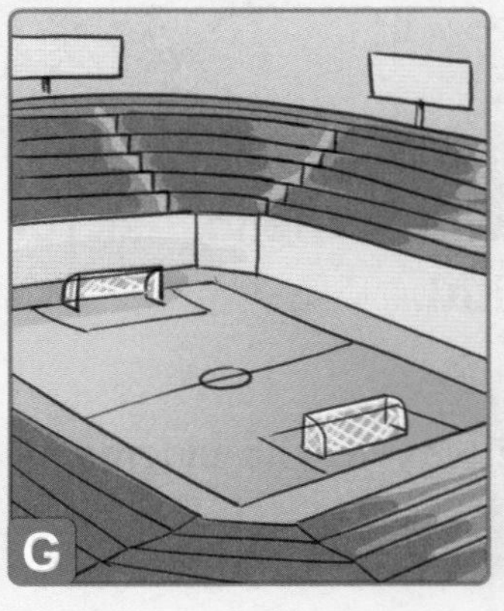

Speaking Part 1

2 111 **Find the differences.**

There are ten differences between the two pictures, but you only have to find six.

A

B

3 **Now watch the video and talk about your answers.**

It happened in the past

1 112 **Look, listen and point. Did they find the people?**

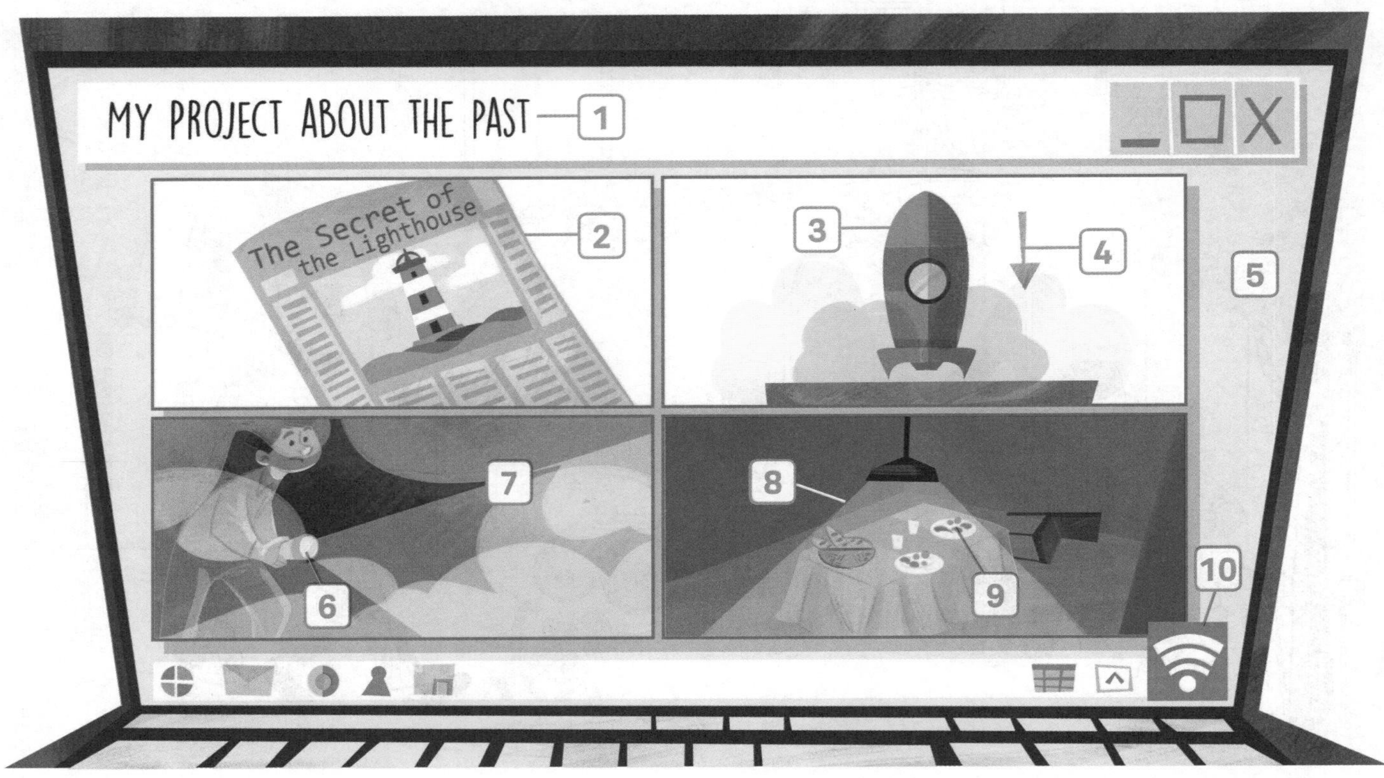

2 113 **Write the numbers. Listen, check and say.**

project	1	wifi	
spaceship		land	
fog		torch	
newspaper		meal	
light		screen	

3 114 **Complete. Use the letters in circles to answer the question. Listen, check and say.**

1. You need this to look at a website. _ ◯ _ _
2. You can read the news in it. ◯ _ _ _ _ _ _ _ _
3. It's something you use to see in the dark. ◯ _ _ _ _
4. It travels to space. _ _ _ _ ◯ _ _ _ _
5. George has to do this for his English homework. _ ◯ _ _ _ _ _
6. The part of a computer where you can see words or pictures. _ _ _ _ _ ◯
7. Breakfast is an example of this. _ ◯ _ _
8. I know my friend is in his room, because the _ _ _ _ ◯ is on.

What was George using for his project? The _ _ _ _ _ _ _ _

4 115 **Circle the correct words. Listen, check and say.**

There wasn't **anyone / no-one** inside. There was (1) **anyone / no-one** there. The police looked (2) **everywhere / everyone** but the men weren't (3) **anywhere / nowhere**. They were (4) **anywhere / nowhere** on the island. Was (5) **anything / nothing** missing? No. Perhaps a spaceship took them (6) **nowhere / somewhere**.

Look & Learn

everything **everywhere** everyone
anything **anywhere** **anyone**
nothing **nowhere** **no-one**
something **somewhere** someone

5 116 **Read and complete. Listen, check and say.**

improved • invented • online • news • information • find out

Katy Do you know who (1) invented the first computer? I'd love to (2) __________.

David We've got a computer here. Let's go (3) __________! Look. You can find (4) __________ about anything on the internet.

Katy I know! How did people know what was happening in the world before the internet?

David They had to buy newspapers, listen to the radio or watch the (5) __________ on TV! The internet changed everything.

Katy Yes, it did. But do you think the internet has (6) __________ our lives?

David Hmm. That's a good question!

6 Say & Play **Complete the puzzle.**

Student A **Make a sentence with a word in the puzzle, but don't say the word. Say *beep*.**

Student B **Go to page 128. Listen to Student A and find out the missing word.**

Two across:
In which year did someone __________ the computer?

Three down:
I'm hungry. Let's go out for a __________.

1 NEWSPAPER
2 INVENT
3 MEAL
4 SPACESHIP
5 S
6
7 L
8
9 ONLINE
10 L

It happened in the past

7 117 Listen and read. Who ate the picnic?

Sarah It's time for our picnic, George. Oh, where's the food?
George I was carrying our picnic up to the tree house when I dropped it.

Sarah What happened?
George I invented a way to bring the picnic into the tree house! I put it all in a box.

George I was pulling the box up when suddenly it broke. Max was walking past when the food fell on him. He ran away.
Sarah Oh no! Poor Max!

George I looked for him everywhere. When I found him, he was eating our sandwiches!
Sarah Ha, ha! Max always loves picnics!

8 Read and match.

Look & Learn

I **was pulling** the box up when it **broke**.
He **was walking** under the tree house when the box **fell** on top of him.

Past continuous (interrupted actions) p. 140

1 I was running for the bus
2 He was walking the dog
3 They were watching the match
4 I was opening the window
5 She was listening to the radio
6 You were waiting on the platform

a when their team scored.
b when she heard the news.
c when I saw you.
d when I fell over.
e when it ran away.
f when a bird flew in.

9 🔊118 Choose the correct words. Listen and check.

1
Nick Hi Emma. I'm sorry I'm late.
Emma What happened?
Nick I (**was cycling**) / **cycled** past the car factory when a fire (1) **was starting** / **started**. I had to wait until the fire engine came.

2
Ben That's a really old newspaper! Where did you find it?
Ann My grandma (2) **was tidying** / **tidied** her house when she (3) **was finding** / **found** it in an old box. Look at the date! It's from 70 years ago.
Ben Wow! That's amazing.

3
Charlie Guess who I saw today? A famous actor! I (4) **was looking** / **looked** for a book in the bookshop when she (5) **was coming** / **came** in.
Grace Did you say hello?
Charlie No, I didn't. She (6) **was talking** / **talked** to someone on her phone.

10 Write sentences. Use the Past continuous and Past simple. Then write the correct number in the boxes.

have a picnic / start to rain

1 We were having a picnic when it started to rain.

drawing a picture / pencil break

2 I ______________________________.

look at the screen / fall over

3 She ______________________________

have dinner / grandma phone

4 They ______________________________.

A ☐

B ☐

C 1

D ☐

11 Say & Play Work in pairs. Take two cards and make a sentence using the Past continuous and the Past simple.

I was playing on the beach when I saw an octopus.

FLYERS PRACTICE

Speaking Part 3

1 119 **Look at the pictures. Listen and continue to tell the story.**

Remember to talk about the pictures in the present.

HOLLY AND BEN FIND SOMETHING

2 **Now watch the video and talk about your answers.**

Reading and Writing Part 3

3 Read the story. Choose a word from the box. Write the correct word next to numbers 1-5. There is one example.

To choose the best name for the story, think about everything that happens in the story, not just some things.

example interesting	boring	screen	anywhere	missing
landed	nowhere	online	torch	saw

This is an interesting story about a woman, Helen White, who lost an expensive ring. Many years ago, Helen was washing the plates after dinner one night when she saw that her ring was **(1)** ___________. 'Perhaps I lost it when I was working in the garden,' she thought, so she went outside to look for it.
It was dark so she took her **(2)** ___________. She looked everywhere but she couldn't find it **(3)** ___________. She felt very sad because it was a very special ring.
Fifty years later, Helen's grandchildren were playing in the garden when they **(4)** ___________ something silver.
It was the ring! Helen was very, very pleased to see it again. I found the story **(5)** ___________. It was on a news website. It's a great story, isn't it?

(6) Now choose the best name for the story. Tick one box.

Mrs White's grandchildren ☐ The missing ring ☐ In the newspaper ☐

15 I love my job

1 🔊120 **Look, listen and point. What was the newspaper story about?**

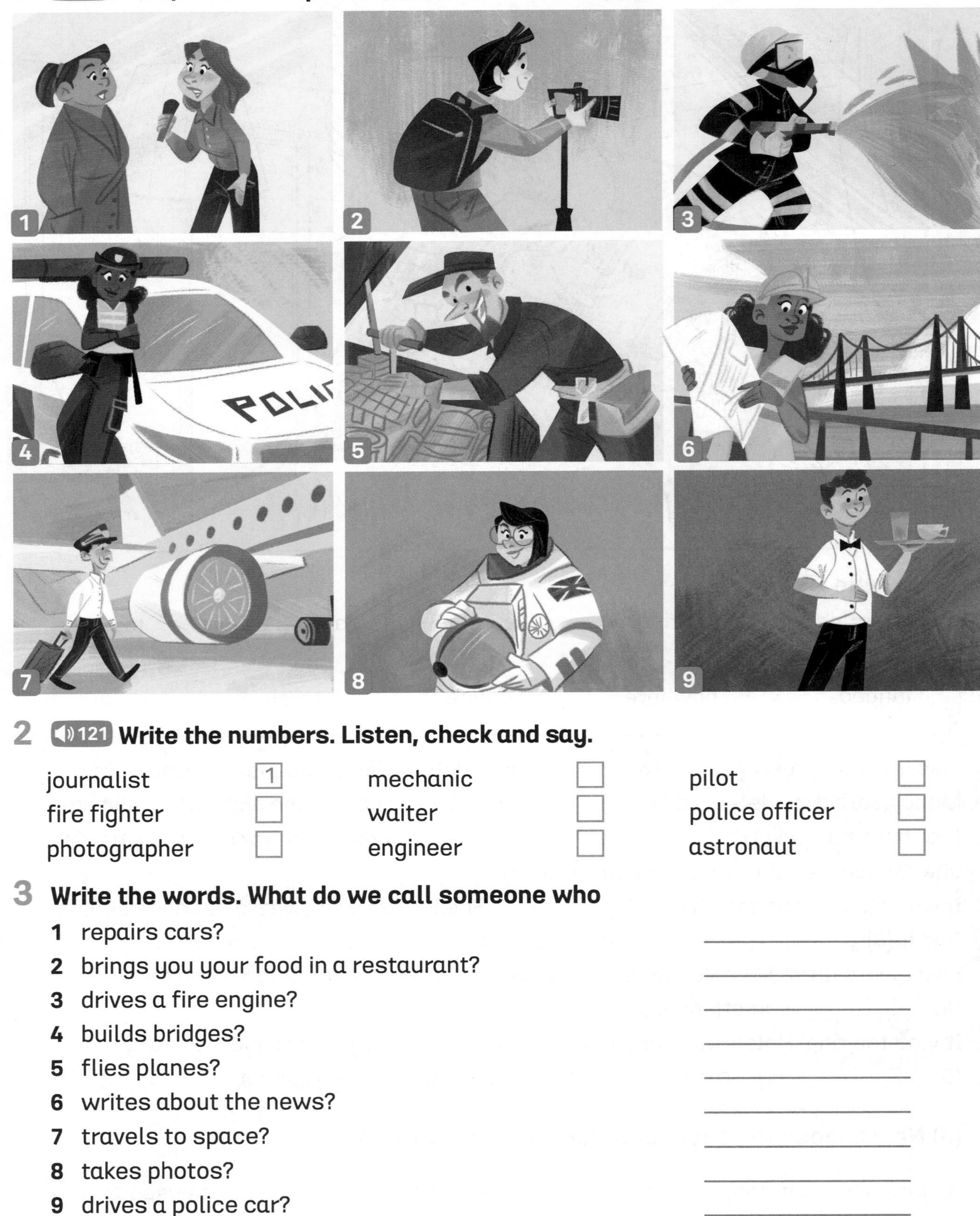

2 🔊121 **Write the numbers. Listen, check and say.**

journalist	1	mechanic	☐	pilot	☐
fire fighter	☐	waiter	☐	police officer	☐
photographer	☐	engineer	☐	astronaut	☐

3 **Write the words. What do we call someone who**

1. repairs cars? ________________
2. brings you your food in a restaurant? ________________
3. drives a fire engine? ________________
4. builds bridges? ________________
5. flies planes? ________________
6. writes about the news? ________________
7. travels to space? ________________
8. takes photos? ________________
9. drives a police car? ________________

4 🔊122 Look and choose. Then listen and check. Say the words.

1 These are **flats / offices**.
2 She's a **designer / teacher**.
3 He's a **mechanic / businessman**.
4 She's a **businesswoman / fire fighter**.
5 He's an **engineer / artist**.
6 He's **a teacher / an actor**.
7 She's a **police officer / manager**.
8 He's a **lorry / taxi driver**.

5 🔊123 Say the Sounds Listen. /s/ or /z/? Then say the words three times.

astronaut business designer artist newspaper

Look & Learn

a few ideas
a little time

6 Read and match with the people in exercise 4.

A ☐ My desk is full of paper, pencils, crayons and magazines. I usually get a few ideas from magazines for the clothes I want to design. I like to think about how clothes will feel, and what colours will look nice together.

B ☐ I usually work during the day, but if I've got a little time in the evening, I work then, too. I usually wear old clothes when I work, because I always drop paint on them!

C ☐ I work five days a week, from 9 o'clock to 5 o'clock. I work in a big, busy office. I've got a desk with a computer and a phone. Oh, that's my manager. She wants to talk to me about a few things. See you later!

D ☐ I usually work in the theatre. I sometimes work on TV and then I can save a little money. I prefer the theatre.

7 Say & Play What's my job? Ask and answer.

Do you work in an office?

Do you help people?

Are you a ....?

No, I don't.

Yes, I do.

15 I love my job

8 🔊124 Listen and read. Does Sarah want to be a teacher?

Sarah That's a great camera.
George Yes, it's my dad's. I want to learn how to take good photos. Then one day, perhaps I will be a famous photographer.

Sarah Will you take photos of the city?
George No, I won't.
Sarah Will you take photos of wild animals?
George Yes, I will. What will you be when you are a grown-up?

Sarah Well, I like English and writing. I might be a teacher or I might be a journalist. I don't like art so I won't be a designer.

George Perhaps we'll travel around the world and write a book about the places we visit. I'll take the photos and you'll write the stories.
Sarah That's a great idea! It will be a cool job!

9 Read again and circle the answer.

1 Will George be a famous photographer?
Yes, he will. / No, he won't. / (He might.)

2 Will he take photos of the city?
Yes, he will. / No, he won't. / He might.

3 Will Sarah work in a school?
Yes, she will. / No, she won't. / She might.

4 Will she be a designer?
Yes, she will. / No, she won't. / She might.

5 Will George and Sarah write a book?
Yes, they will. / No, they won't. / They might.

Look & Learn

Will you take photos of the city?
Yes, I **will**. No, I **won't**.
I **will** be a famous photographer.
I **won't** be a designer.
I **might** be a journalist.

▶ *will / might* p. 141

10 🔊125 **What jobs will / won't they do? Listen and write the information.**

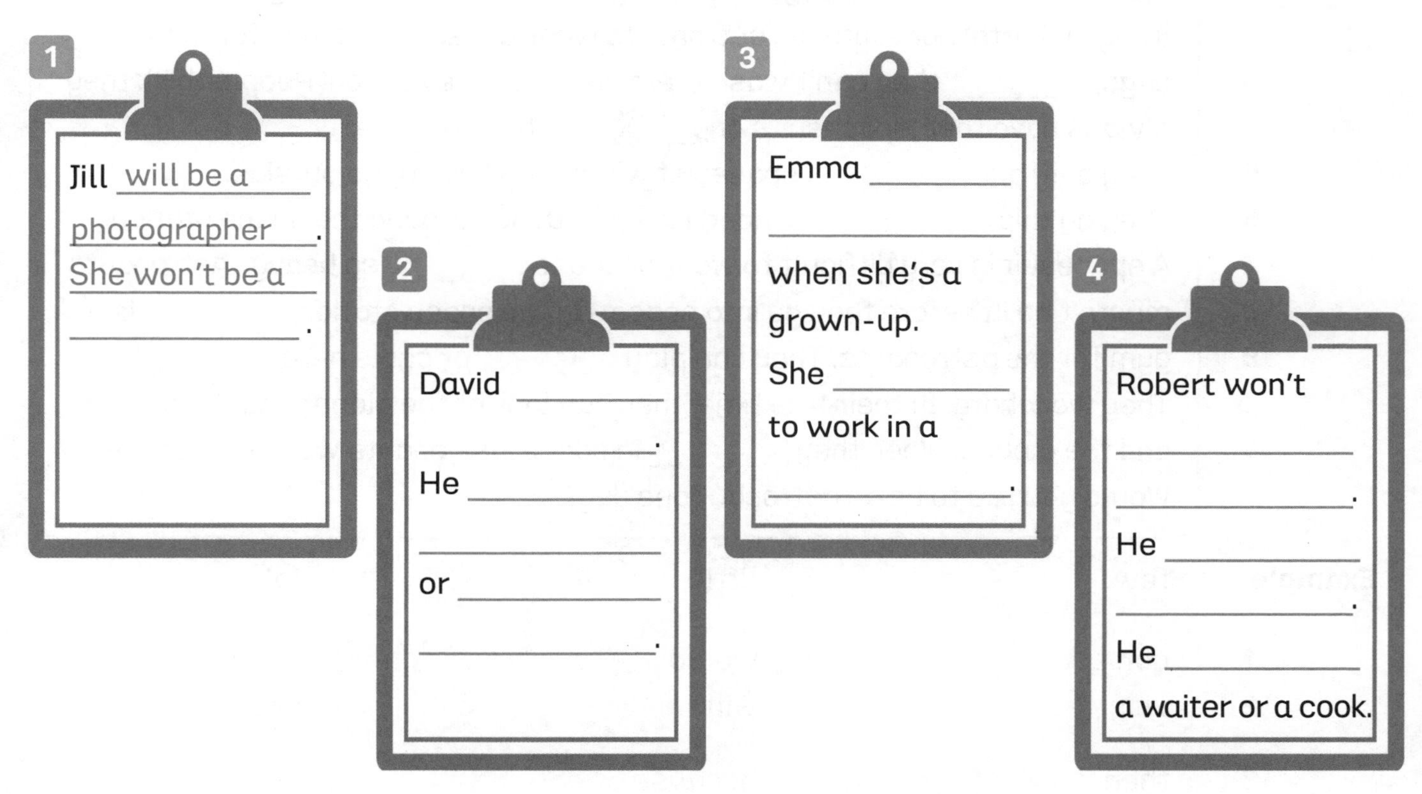

11 **What about you? Ask and answer.**

What job will you do one day?

What will you do in your job?

How will you get to work?

Where will you work?

15 FLYERS PRACTICE

Reading and Writing Part 4

1 Read the text. Choose the right words and write them on the lines.

Think about the kind of word you need for each space. Is it an object, or a describing word, or an action word?

A DAY IN THE LIFE OF AN ASTRONAUT

Example Astronauts travel to the Space Station and live there for a few months.
1 They learn about living and working in space. They ________ be there for three
2 months, six months or longer. But living there ________ be very different from living on Earth! For example, astronauts wear the same clothes for many
3 days, ________ they can't wash them on the space station! People think they
4 always have their spacesuits on, ________ this isn't true.
5 They only put ________ a spacesuit when they have to go outside.
6 They do this ________ they need to repair things around the space station.
7 A spacesuit is very difficult to wear because ________ so heavy. Astronauts
8 mustn't be ill before they go into space. On the space station, ________ is a
9 gym for the astronauts. They can play ________ or cycle here. They work hard. In their free time, they can look at the planet and the oceans
10 and the clouds. When they ________ in space, astronauts work in an office. Would you like to be an astronaut one day?

Example	few	little	lot
1	don't	would	might
2	was	will	are
3	then	because	so
4	so	or	but
5	on	out	up
6	what	when	who
7	it's	he's	his
8	their	there	they're
9	sports	music	chess
10	are	can't	aren't

Speaking Part 2

2 126 **Ask questions to find the missing information. Student A look at this page, Student B look at page 129.**

Think about the questions to ask. Are they *Wh*-questions *Where / What / Who / Which* (or *How*) or *Yes/No* questions?

Student A

Grace's mum goes to work

Job	manager
Work in an office	yes
Travel to work	She goes by bus.
Time start	9 o'clock in the morning
Interesting	yes

Harry's dad goes to work

Job	?
Work in an office	?
Travel to work	?
Time start	?
Interesting	?

Speaking Part 4

3 Ask and answer the questions with your partner.

1. What's your favourite subject at school?
2. What subjects are you good at?
3. What's the most exciting job you know about?
4. Where will you live when you are a grown-up?
5. Would you like to be an astronaut?

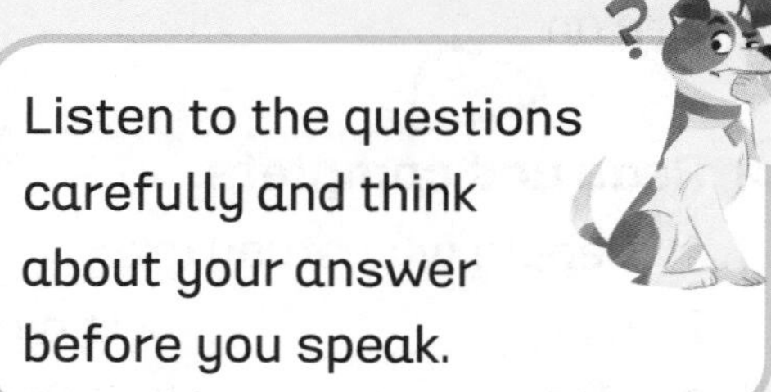

Listen to the questions carefully and think about your answer before you speak.

4 **Now watch the video and talk about your answers.**

16 Let's watch TV!

1 127 **Look, listen and point. What did Max do?**

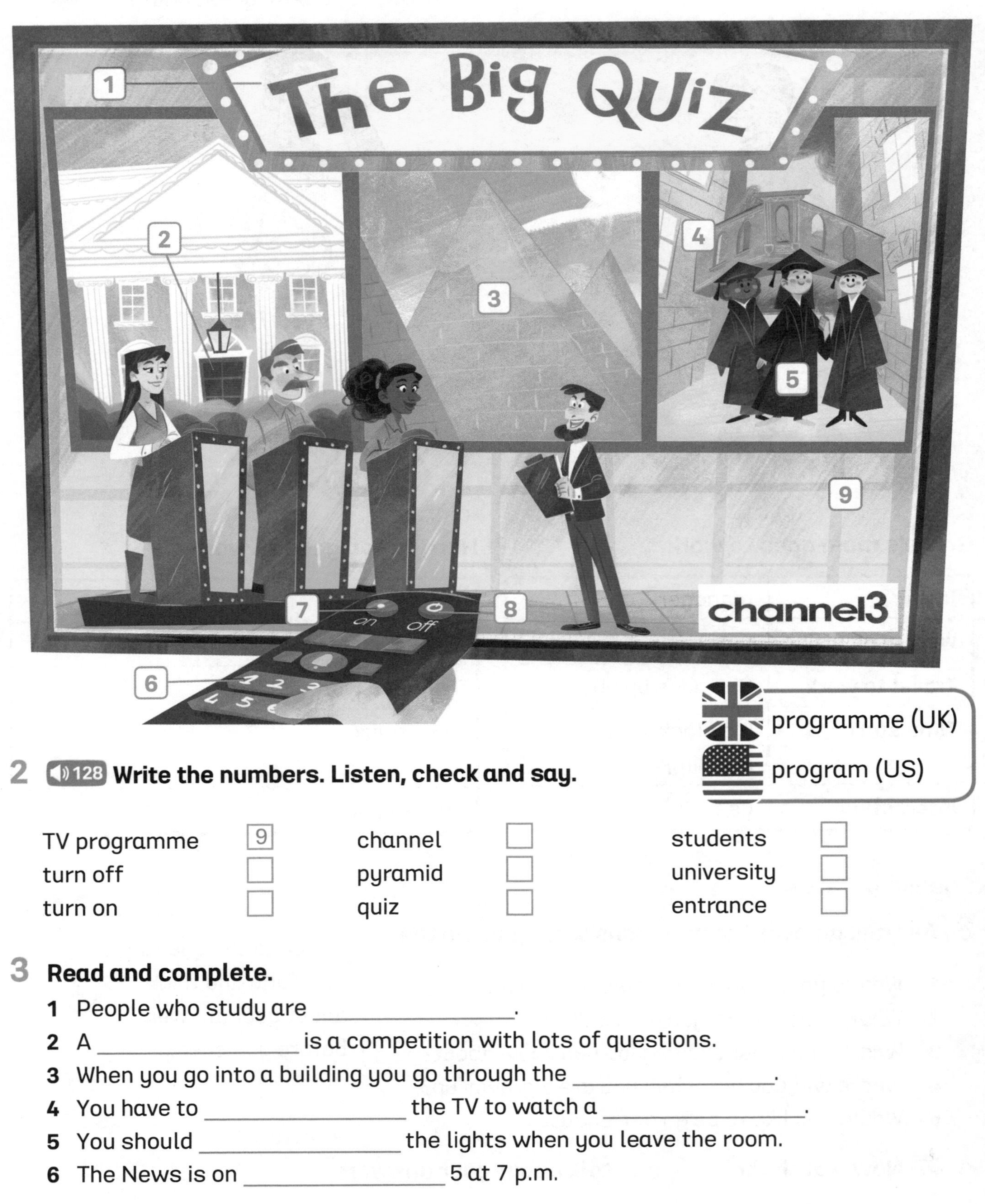

programme (UK)
program (US)

2 128 **Write the numbers. Listen, check and say.**

TV programme	9	channel	☐	students	☐
turn off	☐	pyramid	☐	university	☐
turn on	☐	quiz	☐	entrance	☐

3 Read and complete.

1 People who study are ________________.
2 A ________________ is a competition with lots of questions.
3 When you go into a building you go through the ________________.
4 You have to ________________ the TV to watch a ________________.
5 You should ________________ the lights when you leave the room.
6 The News is on ________________ 5 at 7 p.m.

4 129 **Read and circle. Then listen and check. Say the words.**

If you never do anything exciting and you're feeling (**1**) **wonderful / bored**, why not watch The Big Quiz? It's new and very (**2**) **interested / popular** with young people. It's really fun and never (**3**) **boring / wonderful**. You'll be (**4**) **frightened / interested** to learn new things. There are several questions. Some of the questions are really (**5**) **interesting / enormous**. Last week, the first question was about the blue whale. Did you know this creature is about 30 metres long? It's (**6**) **enormous / popular**! It's (**7**) **frightening / popular** being on TV for the first time, but in the end, everyone loves it and has a (**8**) **boring / wonderful** time.

Look & Learn

You feel	when something is
bored	**boring**
interested	**interesting**
frightened	**frightening**

5 130 **Do the quiz! Listen and check.**

bored • boring • enormous • frightened • frightening
interested • interesting • popular • wonderful

Quiz

1. Which word means the same as *scary*?
2. How do you feel when you see something *scary*?
3. What is the opposite of *boring*?
4. How do you feel when you want to learn new things?
5. How do you feel when something isn't interesting?
6. Which word means *everyone likes it*?
7. Which word means *very good, fantastic*?
8. Which word means *huge*?
9. Which word means *not fun* or *not interesting*?

6 Say & Play **Work in pairs and play the game!**

16 Let's watch TV!

7 131 Listen and read. What's on channel 6?

Sarah What shall we watch today?
George There's a film about a monster on channel 4.
Sarah No, thanks! Scary films make Max frightened.

Sarah OK. There's a cooking programme on channel 6. Let's watch it.
George OK, but cooking programmes make me hungry!
Sarah Me too! I'll get some olives.

Sarah These olives are delicious.
George Yes, they are, but olives make me thirsty. Have you got anything to drink?

Sarah George! Watching TV makes you lazy. Go and get a glass of water. Then let's turn off the TV and play outside.
George Good idea!

8 Read and match.

1 Scary films
2 Sad songs
3 Singing
4 Too much chocolate
5 Too much salt
6 Going to bed late

a makes me happy.
b makes you ill.
c makes you tired.
d makes you thirsty.
e make Max frightened.
f make me unhappy.

Look & Learn

Scary films **make** Max **frightened**.
Olives **make** me **thirsty**.

make somebody / something + adj p. 141

9 What makes you happy / sad / frightened / hungry / thirsty / angry?

Bad dreams make me frightened.

10 132 Choose and circle. Then listen and check.

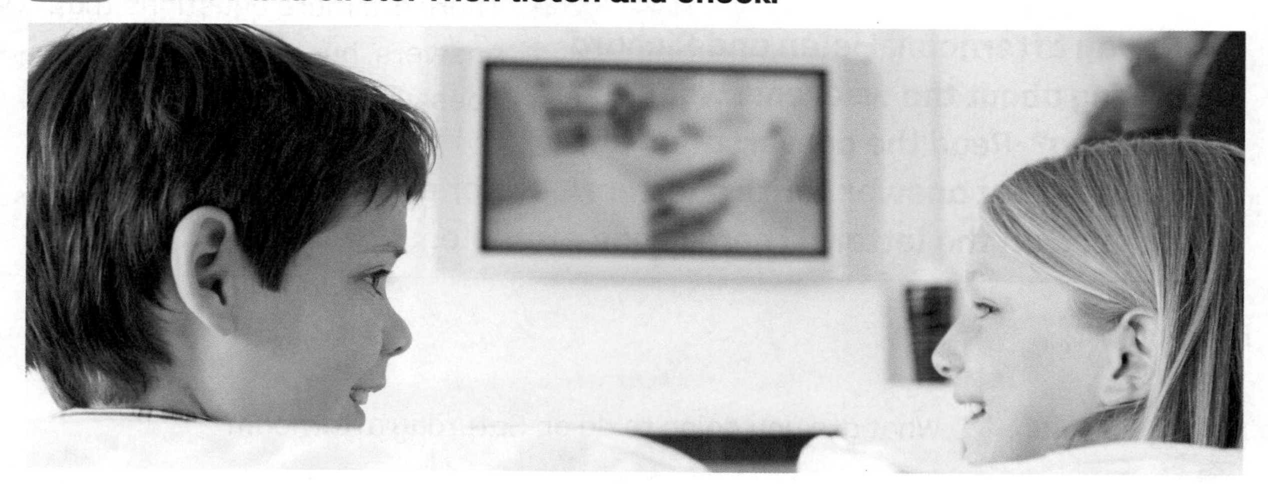

Boy Turn on the TV. I love watching TV after school.
Girl (1) **Me too. / I don't agree.** It makes me happy.
Boy Shall we watch Maisy Mouse on channel 2 or Quiz Time on channel 5?
Girl Let's watch Maisy Mouse. It's better than Quiz Time.
Boy (2) **I agree. / I don't agree.** Quiz Time is much better than Maisy Mouse. And it's more popular.
Girl (3) **I agree. / I don't agree.** Everybody loves Maisy Mouse. It's funnier than Quiz Time.
Boy (4) **I agree. / I don't agree.** Quiz Time isn't as funny as Maisy Mouse, but it's more interesting.
Girl Well, we don't agree, so let's turn off the TV and play a game instead!
Boy But which game shall we play?

11 Write the same thing in a different way.

1 Maths isn't as interesting as science.
Science is more interesting than maths.
2 Snowboarding is more exciting than skiing.
______
3 Quizzes aren't as important as cooking programmes.
______
4 Cats aren't as popular as dogs.
______
5 Snakes are more frightening than spiders.
______

12 Say & Play Talk with a friend. Compare different school subjects, sports and TV programmes. Do you and your friend agree?

Art isn't as easy as science.

I disagree! I think science is more difficult than art.

16 FLYERS PRACTICE

Reading and Writing Part 2

1 It's Friday afternoon. Helen and Richard are talking about the weekend. What does Richard say? Read the conversation and choose the best answer. Write a letter (A–H) for each answer. You do not need to use all the letters. There is one example.

There are more questions than answers, but only one answer goes with each question.

Example

Helen: What are you going to do on Saturday afternoon?

Richard: C

Questions

1 **Helen:** Then what are you going to do?
Richard: ____________________

2 **Helen:** Which channel is it on?
Richard: ____________________

3 **Helen:** What time does it start?
Richard: ____________________

4 **Helen:** Are you going to have dinner in front of the TV?
Richard: ____________________

5 **Helen:** Who do you think will win the match?
Richard: ____________________

A I'm going to watch the football match on TV.
B Yes. It's more interesting than basketball.
~~**C**~~ I'm going to play football in the park after lunch. **(example)**
D It's on channel 1.
E No. I can't eat and watch football. It's too exciting!
F No, I don't think they'll win.
G It starts at 7 o'clock.
H I think my team will win. That'll make me happy.

Reading and Writing Part 6

2 Read the letter and write the missing words. Write one word on each line.

Read to the end of each sentence before you write the missing word.

Dear Sophia,

Example Today my sister Holly had to stand on the ___stage___ in front of 200 people and sing her favourite song. Why? Because she was in a singing

1 competition __________ school. There were several good singers in the

2 competition but my sister __________ the first prize. She wants to be a

3 singer so it made __________ very happy.

4 The prize is a trip __________ London where she will sing in a concert

5 with the winners from other schools. They're __________ to make a TV programme of the concert. I hope you can watch it. It's going to be on channel 3 in December.

From

Frank

REVISION 13-16

1 Find the words for the pictures. Use the letters in the orange squares to spell another job. _ _ _ _ _ _ _ _ _ _ _

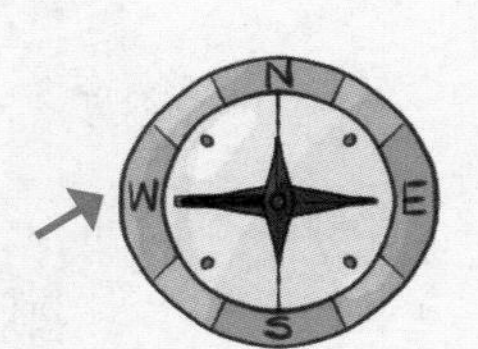

J	A	S	T	R	O	N	A	U	T
O	K	Y	X	J	P	Q	W	L	V
U	Z	W	C	A	S	T	L	E	S
R	E	S	T	A	U	R	A	N	T
N	G	W	D	W	Q	M	Y	R	A
A	D	E	P	Y	R	A	M	I	D
L	X	S	P	I	L	O	T	H	I
I	P	T	O	F	F	I	C	E	U
S	F	J	X	L	I	G	H	T	M
T	Q	V	T	O	R	C	H	U	J

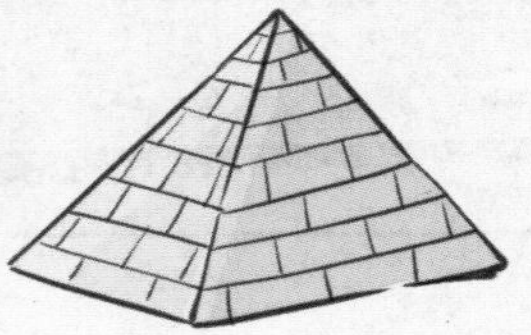

2 Read and complete.

anywhere • boring • everywhere • frightened • information • missing
no-one • police station • restaurant • waiter

Yesterday morning, Mrs Wilson phoned the **(1)** ____________. She spoke to a police officer. 'I'm worried about my cat, Gordo. He's **(2)** ____________.
I've looked **(3)** ____________ but I can't find him **(4)** ____________,' she said.

The police officer made posters and put them on trees in the village.
But **(5)** ____________ had any **(6)** ____________ about the cat, Gordo.

Then one night, a **(7)** ____________ heard a noise in the kitchen in *Yum Yum*, the **(8)** ____________ where he worked.
There was no-one there. He felt **(9)** ____________.
But it was only Gordo! He was inside the bin, eating pizza!

'I think Gordo's food was **(10)** ____________,'
Mrs Wilson said. 'He prefers the food at *Yum Yum*!'

3 **Watch the video. Then answer the questions.**

1 What place did Sarah and her mum want to visit?
2 Why did they want to go there?
3 Where were they staying on holiday?
4 What did they see when they were getting on the bus?
5 What will they bring with them next time?

A visit to the museum

4 **Write about you.**

1 Have you ever visited a museum? ______________________
2 Name three places near your home. ______________________
3 What makes you happy? ______________________
4 What makes you bored? ______________________
5 Where will you go on holiday next year? ______________________

5 Say & Play **Work in pairs. Say what these people were doing when the spaceship landed.**

A family was having a meal when the spaceship landed.

when...

FLYERS PRACTICE TEST

Listening Part 1

133 **Listen and draw lines. There is one example.**

Listening Part 2

134 **Listen and write. There is one example.**

MUM, THE COLLEGE PHONED TODAY...

	About a:	job
1	For a:	______
2	On:	______ June
3	Address:	140 ______ Street
4	Where:	opposite the ______
5	Starts at:	______

FLYERS PRACTICE TEST

Listening Part 3

135 **Where did Holly get each of these things? Listen and write a letter in each box. There is one example.**

Listening Part 4

136 **Listen and tick (✔) the box. There is one example.**

Where is Ben going?

A 

B  ✔

C 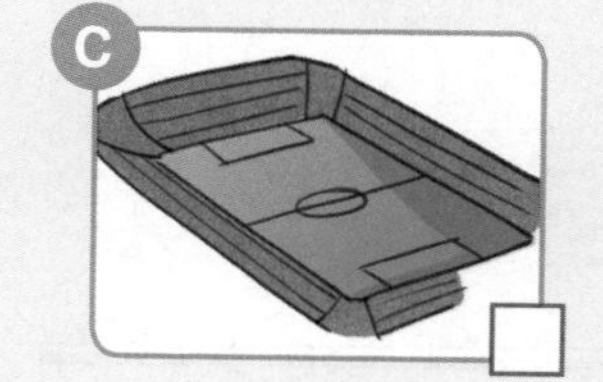

1 What is Ben going to wear?

A 

B 

C 

2 How is Ben going to get there?

A 

B 

C 

3 What time does it start?

A 

B 

C 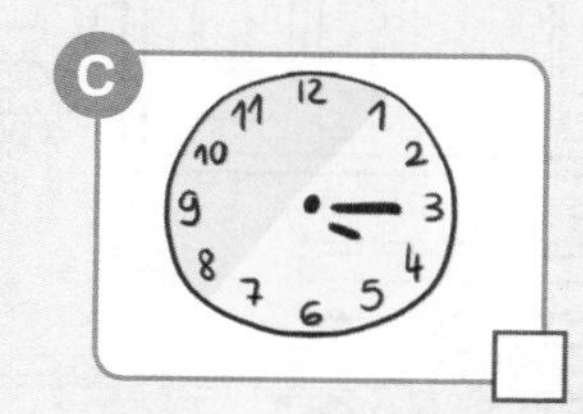

4 What did Ben do with his friends?

A 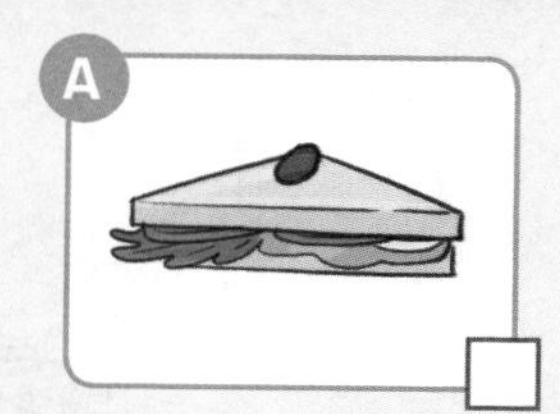

B 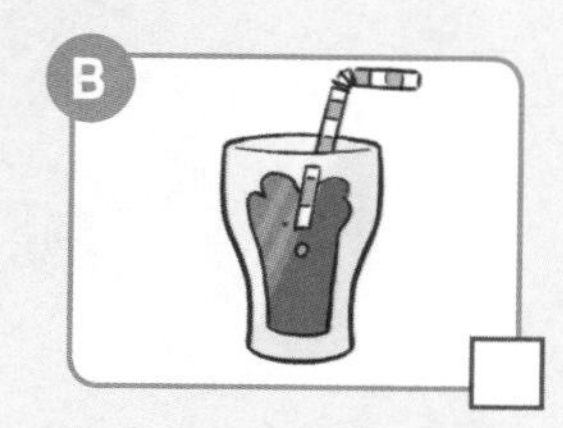

C 

5 What is Ben going to do tomorrow?

A 

B 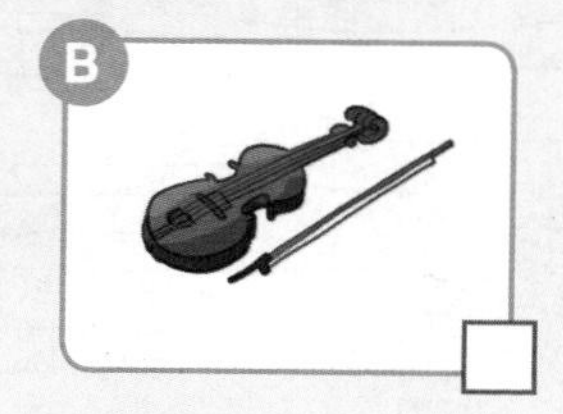

C 

Listening Part 5

137 **Listen and colour and write. There is one example.**

Reading and Writing Part 1

Look and read. Choose the correct words and write them on the lines. There is one example.

a file | a journalist | a tent | a torch | gloves | an elbow | a chemist | a platform | a hotel | a necklace | history | a hospital | planets | a bracelet | a businessman

This is where you keep your work on your computer. You can open and close it. a file

1 These are something you wear on your hands when it is cold. ____________

2 This person works in an office and writes stories for a newspaper. ____________

3 This is where people stand when they are waiting for a train at the station. ____________

4 This is made of gold, silver or plastic. You wear it around your neck. ____________

5 This is between your hand and your shoulder. ____________

6 You can sleep outside in this. ____________

7 This is something you use to see in the dark. You can turn it on to get the light. ____________

8 If you are feeling ill and you need to buy some medicine, you go to this shop. ____________

9 These are in space. There are eight of them. Earth is one of them. ____________

10 This is something you study at school. You learn about the past. ____________

FLYERS PRACTICE TEST

Reading and Writing Part 2

Frank is talking to Betty about what they are doing at the weekend.
What does Frank say? Read the conversation and choose the best answer.
Write a letter (A-H) for each answer. You do not need to use all the letters.
There is one example.

Example

Frank: It's the football competition on Saturday.

Betty: G

Questions

1 **Frank:** Yes, it is. Shall I meet you there?
Betty: ____________

2 **Frank:** I could come to your house if you like.
Betty: ____________

3 **Frank:** It starts at 3 o'clock. We mustn't be late.
Betty: ____________

4 **Frank:** We eat pizza with the team. I love pizza.
Betty: ____________

5 **Frank:** You do like football, don't you?
Betty: ____________

A So do I. It's horrible.
B I don't know where the stadium is.
C Yes, of course I do.
D I don't like football.
E Good idea. Then we can go together.
F So do I. It's my favourite food.
G Is it at the stadium in the town?
H Let's go by bus. What do we do if we win?

Reading and Writing Part 3

Read the story. Choose a word from the box. Write the correct word next to numbers 1-5. There is one example.

example				
played	so	yesterday	broken	team
if	tomorrow	group	taxi	ambulance

Last Friday, Sophia and her friends ___played___ volleyball at the sports centre with their teacher. They were practising for the school competition on Saturday. 'I hope we win the prize', Sophia said. 'I think we're the best **(1)** ____________.'
Suddenly there was a problem. Sophia was jumping for the ball when she fell. She hurt her hand. 'Can you move your fingers?' asked the teacher. 'I can't move my little finger. I think it's **(2)** ____________. What should I do?' said Sophia. 'You should go to the hospital. I don't think we need an **(3)** ____________. I can give you a lift.' The teacher phoned Sophia's parents and they met them at the hospital. 'Look at the x-ray. You can see your finger isn't broken,' said the doctor. 'It's sore **(4)** ____________ you need to take some medicine. But you can play in the competition **(5)** ____________.' Everyone was happy!

(6) Now choose the best name for the story. Tick one box.

Sophia wins the competition ☐ Sophia hurts her finger ☐ A trip in an ambulance ☐

FLYERS PRACTICE TEST

Reading and Writing Part 4

Read the text. Choose the right words and write them on the lines.

Example	The black bear is ___a___ beautiful creature.
1	It isn't as big ____________ a polar bear which people say is the
2	____________ bear in the world. Black bears eat different kinds
3	____________ plants and grass. They also eat fruit and they like
4	____________ fish.
5	The black bear has a lot of fur, ____________ keeps it warm in the winter when it is cold. Their fur can also be different colours, for example black,
6	brown ____________ sometimes white! Black bears usually live in forests
7	and they can climb trees. They can ____________ run quite fast. Black
8	bears ____________ not to meet people and they can be dangerous
9	____________ they are surprised or if they have a baby bear with them. Black bears make their homes in caves. During the summer and autumn,
10	they eat a lot of food and then in the winter they ____________ in their cave. They wake up in spring when the snow disappears. It's an exciting time as they go looking for food because they are very hungry after many months asleep.

Example	a	an	some
1	like	than	as
2	largest	larger	large
3	of	for	in
4	eat	eating	eats
5	which	where	who
6	so	or	if
7	too	and	also
8	prefer	mind	like
9	if	for	to
10	asleep	sleep	sleeps

Reading and Writing Part 5

Look at the picture and read the story. Write some words to complete the sentences about the story. You can use 1, 2, 3 or 4 words.

A TRIP TO LONDON

My name's Helen. I live in a small village with my younger brother and my mum and dad. My brother's name is Harry. Last Sunday, my parents took us to London.
We were very excited. Harry's best friend came too. His name is Michael. We went to the station and caught the train to London.
We went to a science museum first because my dad is interested in space and planets. We went into a dark room and watched a film about the planets. Then we went inside a spaceship and an astronaut told us about how she lives and eats in space. 'How do you sleep in space? Do you have a bed?' asked Harry. 'We do, but there is no up or down in space and we can sleep anywhere. We glue our bed to the wall!' the astronaut said. I was very surprised.
Then we went by bus to London Zoo. Harry's favourite animals are penguins. It took us 20 minutes to find them! But we had a great time watching them. A large penguin jumped out of the water. Then a small penguin jumped out of the water, much higher than the first. Harry shouted, 'Look at the penguins. The penguins are jumping out of the water!' and a penguin jumped out and landed on Harry! We all laughed.

Examples

Helen and her family live in <u>a small village</u>.
The name of Helen's <u>brother</u> is Harry.

Questions

1 Helen and her family went to London ______________________.
2 Harry's friend is called ______________________.
3 They went ________________ to London.
4 Helen's dad likes space and planets ________________ they visited the science museum.
5 Helen was ________________ when she learnt about where astronauts sleep.
6 After 20 minutes, they ______________________.
7 When Harry ________________, a penguin landed on him.

FLYERS PRACTICE TEST

Reading and Writing Part 6

Read the postcard and write the missing words. Write one word on each line.

Dear Emma,

Example: I ___am___ having a great time at the beach. The weather has been fantastic – hot and sunny. Yesterday morning my sister Katy went

1 __________ at the market.

2 She bought __________ sunglasses because she lost hers.

3 I went swimming by __________. Mum was watching from the beach.

4 She wanted to __________ sure I was safe. In the afternoon we all went to a big market. There was a beautiful necklace made of silver. I wanted

5 to buy it but it was __________ expensive. I must find a cheaper one!!

Love

Zoe

Reading and Writing Part 7

Look at the three pictures. Write about this story. Write 20 or more words.

FLYERS PRACTICE TEST

Speaking Part 1

138 **Find the differences.**

A

B

Speaking Part 2

139 **Ask questions to find the missing information. Student A look at this page. Student B look at page 130.**

Betty's holiday

Where?	?
Who / with?	?
How long?	?
hotel?	?
What / do?	?

Oliver's holiday

Where?	mountains
Who / with?	mum and dad
How long?	two weeks
hotel?	farm
What / do?	climb

FLYERS PRACTICE TEST

Speaking Part 3

140 **Listen. Then continue to tell the story.**

A SURPRISE!

Speaking Part 4

141 **Listen and answer the questions.**

Unit 1 • page 7, exercise 5

Unit 2 • page 15, exercise 11

Student B

Say hello	Hello / Hi (*name*)
Respond to suggestion	Yes, great! / That sounds like a good idea.
Respond to offer	Yes, please. / Yes! I love ...
Agree/Suggest another time	OK. / No, let's meet ...
Say goodbye	Bye, see you later / tomorrow / on Friday.

Unit 3 • page 19, exercise 6

Speaking cards

Unit 5 • page 37, exercise 2

Student B

Robert's favourite place

Favourite place	library
Where	at school
Time open	9 a.m.
Like doing	reading comics
When	at lunch time

Holly's favourite place

Favourite place	?
Where	?
Time open	?
Like doing	?
When	?

Unit 6 • page 41, exercise 13

Student B

Take turns. Read a sentence beginning. Can your friend finish the sentence?

Beginnings	Endings
I can't go to school today	because it isn't windy enough.
I can't see	because it's too tall.
I didn't buy that game	because the water is too cold.
I can't wear these shoes	because it isn't loud enough.
I feel tired today	because it was too hot.
He didn't finish the book	because I'm not old enough.

Unit 8 • page 53, exercise 11

Student B

Say what's wrong	I cut my knee / hurt my hand / broke my leg / burnt my arm
Say what happened	I fell off my bike / fell over / fell off a horse / cooked dinner
Respond to advice	Good idea! / No, I don't need to do that.
Say goodbye	Bye, see you later / tomorrow / on Friday

Unit 8 • page 54, exercise 1

Student B

William's Sunday

Where	in the kitchen at home
What / happen	cut finger
How	drop knife
Mum or Dad help	Mum
Call ambulance	no

Helen's Sunday

Where	?
What / happen	?
How	?
Mum or Dad help	?
Call ambulance	?

Speaking cards

Unit 10 • page 67, exercise 11

Student B

What was Jack doing yesterday at these times?

7.00 a.m.	____________
8.00 a.m.	have breakfast
8.30 a.m.	____________
11.00 a.m.	play in playground
3.30 p.m.	____________
5.00 p.m.	watch TV
6.30 p.m.	____________
10.00 p.m.	sleep

Unit 12 • page 79, exercise 11

Student B

The moon is ____________ from the Earth.
The smallest ocean is the Arctic ocean.
The highest waterfall is about ____________ high.
The biggest lake is the Caspian Sea.
The longest cave is 663 kilometres long.
The longest beach is ____________ long.

Unit 14 • page 91, exercise 6

Student B

Make a sentence with a word in the puzzle, but don't say the word. Say *beep*.

Six down:
When there's ____________
it's difficult to see
where you are.

Seven across:
The ____________
is on so I can read.

1
2 I
M
3
4 P
5 S
6 F
R
C
O
O
R
7 L I G H 8 T
V
E
9 O
10 L
E
E
R
A
N
C
N
H
D

Unit 15 • page 101, exercise 2

Student B

Grace's mum goes to work

Job	?
Work in an office	?
Travel to work	?
Time start	?
Interesting	?

Harry's dad goes to work

Job	pilot
Work in an office	no
Travel to work	drives to the airport
Time start	sometimes at 5 o'clock in the morning
Interesting	yes

Speaking cards

▶ Practice Test • page 123

Student B

Betty's holiday

Where?	beach
Who / with?	cousins
How long?	one week
hotel?	yes
What / do?	sail

Oliver's holiday

Where?	?
Who / with?	?
How long?	?
hotel?	?
What / do?	?

0 Welcome!

Months

January

February

March

April

May

June

July

August

September

October

November

December

Ordinal numbers

1st – first

2nd – second

3rd – third

4th – fourth

5th – fifth

6th – sixth

7th – seventh

8th – eighth

9th – ninth

10th – tenth

11th – eleventh

12th – twelfth

13th – thirteenth

14th – fourteenth

15th – fifteenth

16th – sixteenth

17th – seventeenth

18th – eighteenth

19th – nineteenth

20th – twentieth

21st – twenty-first

22nd – twenty-second

23rd – twenty-third

24th – twenty-fourth

25th – twenty-fifth

26th – twenty-sixth

27th – twenty-seventh

28th – twenty-eighth

29th – twenty-ninth

30th – thirtieth

31st – thirty-first

Questions & Expressions

When's your birthday?

It's in April.

It's on the 12th of March.

1 It isn't in my room!

Items in the home

bin

brush

comb

cooker

cushion

desk

diary

doll

fridge

gate

key

oven

shampoo

shelf

soap

steps

swing

Wh- questions

What

When

Where

Which

Who

Why

How

Expressions

This is the house where they live.

Wordlist

2 Hide the biscuits!

Food

biscuits ______
bread ______
butter ______
cake ______
cereal ______
cheese ______
chocolate ______
flour ______
honey ______
ice cream ______
jam ______
olives ______
onions ______
pepper ______
pizza ______
salt ______
sandwiches ______
strawberries ______
sugar ______
tomatoes ______
yoghurt ______

Table setting

chopsticks ______
fork ______
glass ______
knife ______
plate ______
spoon ______

Sense verbs

feel like ______
look like ______
smell like ______
sound like ______
taste like ______

Questions & Expressions

Shall we buy some biscuits? ______
What's it like? ______
It's delicious. ______

3 This is your invitation!

Invitations and parties

address ______
balloon ______
Dear ______
envelope ______
husband ______
invitation ______
married ______
members ______
middle ______
post office ______
post ______
stamp ______
street party ______
surname ______
telephone ______
wife ______

Questions & Expressions

We could invite our teacher. ______
What about Sunday? ______

4 Let's dress up!

Clothes & Accessories

belt ______
bracelet ______
crown ______
dress ______
gloves ______
necklace ______
spotted pyjamas ______
striped T-shirt ______
sunglasses ______
trainers ______
umbrella ______
uniform ______

Materials

gold ______
metal ______
plastic ______

silver
wood
wool

Questions & Expressions
What's it made of?
It's made of silver.
I'm wearing a necklace today.

5 My favourite subject!

School
art
dictionary
geography
gym
history
maths
rucksack
science
timetable

Time
a.m.
midday / twelve a.m.
midnight / twelve p.m.
p.m.

6 They are the winners!

Sports
flag
golf
hole
prize
race
score
skis
sledge
snowball
snowboard
snowman
team
volleyball

Expressions
I'm not fast enough.
I'm too short.
If we lose, we buy the other team a pizza.

7 He plays the drums

Music
band
concert
drums
guitar
instruments
noisy
pop music
rock music
singer
tune
violin

Hobbies
collect stamps
do puzzles
draw cartoons
make models
play chess
read magazines

Expressions
He doesn't like playing chess.
I don't mind playing the guitar.
I'm interested in golf.
She likes doing puzzles.

8 Can you move your toes?

Body and health
ambulance
bandage
broken
elbow
fingers
knee
medicine
toes
x-ray

Wordlist

Accidents
break your arm ____
burn your hand ____
cut your finger ____
fall over ____
have a sore toe ____

Questions & Expressions
What should I do? ____
You should take this medicine. ____
Should I wear the bandage at home? ____

9 A storm at night

Seasons
autumn ____
spring ____
summer ____
winter ____

Weather and outside
dark ____
foggy ____
light ____
storm ____
tent ____
warm ____

Holidays
airport ____
camp ____
hotel ____
money ____
suitcase ____
taxi ____

Questions & Expressions
What are you going to do? ____
Where are you going to go? ____
We're going to sleep in the tree house ____

10 What a cool car!

Transport
bicycle ____
fire engine ____
lift ____
motorway ____
passenger ____
platform ____
racing car ____
railway ____
rocket ____
traffic ____
tyre ____
wheel ____

Verbs
cycle ____
drive ____
practise ____
push ____
repair ____

Questions & Expressions
I was riding my bike yesterday ____
What were you doing? ____
I was practising with the band all day. ____

11 What kind of animal is that?

Animals and insects
beetle ____
butterfly ____
camel ____
dinosaur ____
dolphin ____
eagle ____
elephant ____
forest ____
fur ____
insect ____
jungle ____
nest ____
octopus ____

swan
tortoise
wings

Adjectives
extinct
furry
wild

Questions & Expressions
Have you ever ridden a camel?
My mum has swum with dolphins.

12 Our world

The world around us
air
beach
bridge
cave
desert
Earth
fire
hill
land
ocean
path
planet
pond
space
stream
wood

Questions & Expressions
Have you saved the planet yet?
I've already fed the birds.
I've just planted the flowers.

13 Places and directions

Places
bank
castle
chemist
factory
fire station
museum
police station
restaurant
skyscraper
stadium
theatre

Cardinal directions
east
north
south
west

Directions
across the road
in the middle
on the left
on the right
over the bridge
past the school
straight on
through the park
turn left
turn right

Questions & Expressions
Can you tell me the way to the theatre?
Do you know the way to the bank?
Where's the castle?

14 It happened in the past

Getting information
find out
improve
information
invent
land
news
newspaper
online
project
screen
wifi

Wordlist

At home and outside

fog ______
light ______
meal ______
spaceship ______
torch ______

Indefinite pronouns

anyone ______
anything ______
no-one ______
someone ______

Adverbs

anywhere ______
everything ______
nowhere ______
somewhere ______

15 I love my job

Jobs

actor ______
artist ______
astronaut ______
businessman ______
businesswoman ______
designer ______
engineer ______
fire fighter ______
journalist ______
manager ______
mechanic ______
office ______
photographer ______
pilot ______
police officer ______
taxi driver ______
teacher ______
waiter ______

Questions & Expressions

I might be a journalist. ______
I will be a famous photographer. ______
Will you take photos of the city? ______

16 Let's watch TV!

Television

channel ______
entrance ______
pyramid ______
quiz ______
students ______
turn off ______
turn on ______
TV programme ______
university ______

Adjectives

bored ______
boring ______
enormous ______
frightened ______
frightening ______
interested ______
interesting ______
popular ______
wonderful ______

Expressions

I agree. ______
I don't agree. ______
Me too. ______

Grammar tables

where clauses

We use ***where*** to refer to a place.

This is the house **where** they live.
This is the living room **where** they watch TV.

be, feel, look, smell, sound, taste like

What's it **like**?
They **look like** nice biscuits.
It **smells like** strawberries.
It **sounds like** my brother.
This biscuit **tastes like** chocolate.
It **feels like** a ball.

shall

We use ***shall*** to make suggestions.

Shall I buy some snacks?	Yes, please!
Shall we watch a film on TV?	Good idea.

could

We use ***could*** to express possibility.

I **could bring** a cake.
You **could put** the balloons on the tree.
She **could invite** her friends.
They **could write** invitations.

be made of

We use ***be made of*** to talk about materials.

What's it **made of**?
The toy is **made of** wood.
The necklace is **made of** silver.

Grammar tables

Present simple v Present continuous

We use the **Present simple** to talk about what you do **every day / every night / usually / always / sometimes / never**.

We use the **Present continuous** to talk about what you are doing **now / today**.

I don't usually wear a necklace.
I'm wearing a necklace today.

Present simple

AFFIRMATIVE FORM	NEGATIVE FORM	INTERROGATIVE FORM	SHORT ANSWERS
I / you play.	I / you **don't** play.	**Do** I / you play?	Yes, I / you **do**. No, I / you **don't**.
He / She / It play**s**.	He / She / It **doesn't** play.	**Does** he / she / it play?	Yes, he / she / it **does**. No, he / she / it **doesn't**.
We / You / They play.	We / You / They **don't** play.	**Do** we / you / they play?	Yes, we / you / they **do**. No, we / you / they **don't**.

Present continuous

AFFIRMATIVE FORM	NEGATIVE FORM	INTERROGATIVE FORM	SHORT ANSWERS
I**'m** play**ing**.	I**'m not** play**ing**.	**Am** I play**ing**?	Yes, I **am**. No, I**'m not**.
You**'re** play**ing**.	You **aren't** play**ing**.	**Are** you play**ing**?	Yes, you **are**. No, you **aren't**.
He / She / It**'s** play**ing**.	He / She / It **isn't** play**ing**.	**Is** he / she / it play**ing**?	Yes, he / she / it **is**. No, he / she / it **isn't**.
We**'re** play**ing**.	We **aren't** play**ing**.	**Are** we play**ing**?	Yes, we **are**. No, we **aren't**.
You**'re** play**ing**.	You **aren't** play**ing**.	**Are** you play**ing**?	Yes, you **are**. No, you **aren't**.
They**'re** play**ing**.	They **aren't** play**ing**.	**Are** they play**ing**?	Yes, they **are**. No, they **aren't**.

if clause (zero conditional)

We use the ***if*-clause** to talk about things that always happen in a certain situation.
We use the Present simple in both the *if*-clause and the main clause.

If it's sunny, they play football in the park.
If they don't play well, they lose.

Tag questions

We use **tag questions** to confirm or check information.

This is your brother's band, **isn't it**? **He isn't** very good, **is he**?
She can play the drums, **can't she**? **She can't** play the drums, **can she**?
They play the guitar well, **don't they**? **They don't play** the guitar well, **do they**?

should

We use ***should*** to give and ask for advice.

Should I wear a bandage?	**Yes**, you **should.**
	No, you **shouldn't.**
What should I do?	You **should** go to bed early.
	You **shouldn't** play football.

be going to

We use ***be going to*** when we want to talk about something that we plan to do or to talk about predictions.

AFFIRMATIVE FORM	NEGATIVE FORM	INTERROGATIVE FORM	SHORT ANSWERS
I**'m going to** play.	I**'m not going to** play.	**Am** I **going to** play?	Yes, I **am**. / No, I**'m not**.
You**'re going to** play.	You **aren't going to** play.	**Are** you **going to** play?	Yes, you **are**. / No, you **aren't**.
He**'s** / She**'s** / It**'s going to** play.	He / She / It **isn't going to** play.	**Is** he / she / it **going to** play?	Yes, he / she / it **is**. No, he / she / it **isn't**.
We**'re** / You**'re** / They**'re going to** play.	We / You / They **aren't going to** play.	**Are** we / you / they **going to** play?	Yes, we / you / they **are**. No, we / you / they **aren't**.

Grammar tables

Past continuous

AFFIRMATIVE FORM	NEGATIVE FORM	INTERROGATIVE FORM	SHORT ANSWERS
I **was** play**ing**.	I **wasn't** play**ing**.	**Was** I play**ing**?	Yes, I **was**. No, I **wasn't**.
You **were** play**ing**.	You **weren't** play**ing**.	**Were** you play**ing**?	Yes, you **were**. No, you **weren't**.
He / She / It **was** play**ing**.	He / She / It **wasn't** play**ing**.	**Was** he / she / it play**ing**?	Yes, he / she / it **was**. No, he / she / it **wasn't**.
We / You / They **were** play**ing**.	We / You / They **weren't** play**ing**.	**Were** we / you / they play**ing**?	Yes, we / you / they **were**. No, we / you / they **weren't**.

Present perfect with ever / never

To form the Present perfect we use: subject + *have / has* + past participle.

He **has** / **hasn't** swum with dolphins.
They **have** / **haven't** written a book.

To form a question we use: *Have / Has* + subject + *ever* + past participle + ?

Have you **ever seen** a camel?	Yes, I **have**. No, I **haven't**.
Has he / she / it **ever seen** a camel?	Yes, he / she / it **has**. No, he / she / it **hasn't**.

To form a negative sentence we use: subject + *have / has* + *never* + past participle.

I**'ve never been** to London.
She**'s never eaten** noodles.

Present perfect with yet / already / just

We use ***yet*** in questions to ask if something has happened.

Have you **fed** the birds **yet**?	Yes, I **have**. No, I **haven't**.

We use ***already*** to say that something has happened.

He's **already** done his homework.
They've **already** fed the birds.

We use ***just*** to say that something has happened recently.

I**'ve just** fed the birds.
The rain **has just** stopped.

Past continuous (interrupted actions)

We use the Past continuous with the Past simple to talk about two past actions. One action interrupts the other action.

We **were having** dinner **when** grandma **phoned**.

When two actions happen at the same time, we use the Past continuous for both.

I **was reading while** I **was sitting** on the bus.

will

AFFIRMATIVE FORM	NEGATIVE FORM	INTERROGATIVE FORM	SHORT ANSWERS
I / you / he / she / it / we / you / they **will** play.	I / you / he / she / it / we / you / they **won't** play.	**Will** I / you / he / she / it / we / you / they **play**?	Yes, I / you / he / she / it / we / you / they **will**.
			No, I / you / he / she / it / we / you / they **won't**.

might

We use ***might*** to talk about something we are not sure about.

I **might** be a journalist.
He **might** work in a school.

make somebody / something + adjective

Scary films **make** Max **frightened**.
That song **makes** me **happy**.

Grammar tables

Irregular verbs

INFINITIVE	PAST SIMPLE	PAST PARTICIPLE
be	was / were	been
bring	brought	brought
build	built	built
begin	began	begun
break	broke	broken
buy	bought	bought
can	could	-
catch	caught	caught
choose	chose	chosen
come	came	come
cut	cut	cut
do	did	done
draw	drew	drawn
drink	drank	drunk
drive	drove	driven
eat	ate	eaten
fall	fell	fallen
feed	fed	fed

INFINITIVE	PAST SIMPLE	PAST PARTICIPLE
feel	felt	felt
find	found	found
forget	forgot	forgotten
fly	flew	flown
get	got	got
give	gave	given
go	went	gone
grow	grew	grown
have	had	had
hear	heard	heard
hide	hid	hidden
hit	hit	hit
hold	held	held
hurt	hurt	hurt
keep	kept	kept
know	knew	known
learn	learnt / learned	learnt / learned
leave	left	left

INFINITIVE	PAST SIMPLE	PAST PARTICIPLE
let	let	let
lie	lied	lied
lose	lost	lost
make	made	made
mean	meant	meant
meet	met	met
put	put	put
read /ri:d/	read /red/	read /red/
ride	rode	ridden
run	ran	ran
say	said	said
see	saw	seen
sell	sold	sold
send	sent	sent
sing	sang	sung
sit	sat	sat
sleep	slept	slept
smell	smelt	smelt

INFINITIVE	PAST SIMPLE	PAST PARTICIPLE
speak	spoke	spoken
spell	spelt / spelled	spelt / spelled
spend	spent	spent
stand	stood	stood
swim	swam	swum
swing	swung	swung
take	took	taken
teach	taught	taught
tell	told	told
think	thought	thought
throw	threw	thrown
understand	understood	understood
wake (up)	woke (up)	woken (up)
wear	wore	worn
write	wrote	written

Fly!
Preparation for the A2 Flyers
Cambridge English Qualifications
Student's Book
by Viv Lambert and Cheryl Pelteret

Managing Editor: Simona Franzoni
Editors: Sue Jones, Linda Pergolini, Lisa Suett
Art Director: Letizia Pigini
Page design: Sergio Elisei
Page layout: Diletta Brutti
Production Manager: Francesco Capitano
Illustrated by: Marta Comito, Licinia Tozzi
Photos: Shutterstock

Cover
Cover design: Sergio Elisei
Illustrated by: Marta Comito

P.O. Box 6
62019 Recanati
Italy
Tel. +39 071 750701
Fax. +39 071 977851
support@elipublishing.com
www.elipublishing.com

Producing educational materials is a complex procedure. While every effort has been made to ensure the correctness of our materials, experience has shown us that inaccuracies are still possible. Every comment or suggestion that we receive will be valuable to us and will allow us to improve our future publications.
Please write to us at: international@elionline.com

Printed by Tecnostampa – Pigini Group Printing Division
Loreto-Trevi, Italy **22.83.317.0**

ISBN 978-88-536-3294-4